JEFFERSON BETHKE

Praise for *Take Back Your Family*

"Jefferson Bethke and his wife, Alyssa, are the real deal. They practice what they preach. As some of the most intentional parents we know, they've found a proven path for the rest of us to follow. If you care about your family, you've got to read this book. From the first paragraph you'll be hooked. Jeff's writing is vulnerable, fresh, passionate, thoughtful, and practical. Don't miss out on this powerful and provocative message. Your family will thank you."

— DRS. LES AND LESLIE PARROTT, #1 *NEW YORK TIMES* BESTSELLING
AUTHORS, *SAVING YOUR MARRIAGE BEFORE IT STARTS*

"There is no one better to help our families rediscover a new way of living than Jefferson. I have watched him and Alyssa take back their family firsthand and it's altogether a more peaceful, deeply meaningful way to live. God's vision for our families is for our thriving!"

— JENNIE ALLEN, *NEW YORK TIMES* BESTSELLING AUTHOR,
GET OUT OF YOUR HEAD; FOUNDER, IF:GATHERING

"This is the stuff. The Bethkes have spent years honing a vision for a flourishing, Jesus-following family in the modern era, complete with iPhones, remote work, dual incomes, all things soccer, etc. Many well-intentioned families are spiraling out of control into busyness and overactivity, fragmenting into radical individualism, and failing to pass on the most important thing of all: a legacy of discipleship. This book is a road map for the weary family soul. It looks back to lovingly point out where we got off track and looks forward to a better future. Like many, I believe the future is ancient, the way forward is backward, and *Take Back Your Family* drills into an ancient and deep well of wisdom and life."

— JOHN MARK COMER, AUTHOR, *LIVE NO LIES*;
FOUNDER, PRACTICING THE WAY

Take Back Your Family

Take Back Your Family

from the Tyrants of Burnout, Busyness, Individualism, and the Nuclear Ideal

Jefferson Bethke

NELSON
BOOKS

An Imprint of Thomas Nelson

Take Back Your Family

© 2021 Jefferson Bethke

Published in Nashville, Tennessee, by Nelson Books, an imprint of Thomas Nelson. Nelson Books and Thomas Nelson are registered trademarks of HarperCollins Christian Publishing, Inc.

Published in association with Yates & Yates, www.yates2.com.

Thomas Nelson titles may be purchased in bulk for educational, business, fundraising, or sales promotional use. For information, please e-mail SpecialMarkets@ThomasNelson.com.

ISBN 978-1-4002-2179-0 (audiobook)
ISBN 978-1-4002-2178-3 (eBook)
ISBN 978-1-4002-3001-3 (IE)
ISBN 978-1-4002-2176-9 (HC)

Library of Congress Cataloging-in-Publication Data

Names: Bethke, Jefferson, author.
Title: Take back your family : from the tyrants of burnout, chaos, individualism, and the nuclear ideal / Jefferson Bethke.
Description: Nashville, Tennessee : Nelson Books, [2021] | Includes bibliographical references. | Summary: "Jefferson Bethke delivers a powerful critique of the nuclear family ideal and calls for a sweeping new paradigm that brings not only longed-for stability but also radical blessings to the world"-- Provided by publisher.
Identifiers: LCCN 2021007008 (print) | LCCN 2021007009 (ebook) | ISBN 9781400221769 (hardcover) | ISBN 9781400221783 (epub)
Subjects: LCSH: Families--Religious aspects--Christianity. | Families--Religious life. | Families.
Classification: LCC BT707.7 .B48 2021 (print) | LCC BT707.7 (ebook) | DDC 248.4--dc23
LC record available at https://lccn.loc.gov/2021007008
LC ebook record available at https://lccn.loc.gov/2021007009

Printed in the United States of America

21 22 23 24 25 LSC 10 9 8 7 6 5 4 3 2 1

Team Bethke (Alyssa, Kinsley, Kannon, and Lucy)
It's the greatest joy of my life to be on mission with you.

Contents

Choose Your Own Adventure

As someone who was an avid fan of the *Goosebumps* choose-your-own-adventure-style books, I want to give you permission to do the same with this one. There are plenty of family and parenting books in the publishing space, but there aren't a ton that ask the really big questions or peel back the curtain on a multi-century project while also offering a fresh yet ancient paradigm. So I'm offering a brief road map and a few notes to hopefully make this book and your reading experience more enjoyable.

First, I'll cut to the chase. Here is the premise of this book: The drowning, chaos, and burnout that your family—and so many others—is feeling right now have been building for a long time. The Western, hyper-individualistic (and consumer-based) view of family has been eating away at all of us. But rethinking the meaning of family, specifically thinking of it in terms of a team, with all the group identity dynamics that come with that, is how God intended for us to function. That's not to say the individual or the team compete with each other—I believe they are symbiotic, like the DNA double helix. But the team aspect of family has been a missing nutrient for decades, and our families are now starved because of it.

Intriguing? I hope so. This team idea is what this book is all about.

The first five chapters pretty much show how we got here. They are a deep dive into the impact of the Industrial Revolution on families and the myth and history of the nuclear family ideal. Then chapters 6 through 10 are the practical ones, explaining what we can do now to implement the idea of family as a team. Throughout the book you'll also find a few "Family Spotlights" that highlight family teams who are successful in their own ways. They all offer a little insight into how their family works and some encouragement, because once you've been captured by the team idea, it still can look a million different ways for a million different families—and that's the fun and creative part! (Note: though I changed some of the names and details in these spotlights, the spirit of the stories remains the same.) So if you want to bounce around or skip ahead a little, this is your permission to do so, though I do think the end will be best understood by grasping the big ideas in the beginning.

I'll conclude by saying that this book couldn't begin to cover all there is to say about family or about God's design for it. In some places, I might have asked more questions than I've offered answers, but the hope is that you'll be captured by a new vision and realize a better way lies beyond the status quo.

You can find more information and answers to your questions at our website, familyteams.com, which also includes links to our podcasts, videos, courses, and more. Feel free to pop over there as you read.

A Declaration of Independence

Well, let's just come out and say it: I have no business writing the book you are reading right now. A book on family by a thirty-two-year-old with small kids and minimal life experience? It's like a preschooler saying, "Hey, I can count! Let me teach you how to balance a bank account!"

But that's the thing: I'm not trying to teach you anything.

I'm declaring independence.

Independence from the insidious individualized culture we live in that has trickled down to affect every facet of our lives and that has become the poison at the root of just about every family tree.

It doesn't matter if you are a nice and tidy religious family or a rugged nontraditional family or some other version. In the West we have the same rot festering right below the soil—same disease, different plants. And that is the disease of self being the most important thing.

This book is me putting a stake in the ground and saying, "I'm out." Consider this my formal request for independence against the typical Western family story that creates consumption monsters. Built to consume. To hoard. To stockpile. To fight for their rights. To get what's theirs. To only use our family as a launching pad for the individual success of ourselves.

Most of our families look like something out of *Lord of the Flies*. And we feel it. Home isn't a safe place; it's crushing us. We feel overwhelmed and overworked. Chaos is our new normal. But hey, we had at least one cute Instagram-worthy moment at the park with our kids, so that's enough, right?

There has to be a better way. But let's be clear—I'm not teaching you how to start a new country.

Our Founding Fathers declared independence in 1776, but the Constitution didn't come until 1787, eleven years later. The Founding Fathers knew what they *didn't* want to be before they knew what they wanted to be.

The zeal and passion and declaration come first before you have any shot of running a new country. You have to draw a line in the sand. They believed there was something fundamentally wrong with structuring government around a monarchy. And so they rejected it and cast a new vision.

And guess what? They got the same critiques everyone does when they step out in inexperience and young age.

"Ha! Yeah, right. You guys don't know how to start a country."

"You'll fail immediately."

"You all haven't lived enough or long enough to know anything about how the government should work."

And who knows? Perhaps even we would have made that critique of some of our Founding Fathers.

James Monroe (our fifth president) was eighteen when he signed the Declaration of Independence. Alexander Hamilton, the first treasury secretary and an enormously large figure in our country's shaping, was twenty-one. James Madison was twenty-five. And the principle author, Thomas Jefferson, was thirty-three.

They believed there was a new way forward, and they were willing to call out the status quo and believe there could be something better.

This book draws a line in the sand. I know what we don't want, and I know the absolute center of the poison that's killing us all. And I'm rejecting it. There is something more, and there is something better. I see a better vision and a future and a promise found in the ancient text of the Scriptures (the Bible) that call us to a new place.

Join me in finding a completely new yet ancient way to do family. It just might change everything.

ONE

A Recent History of Events

Downtown Jerusalem. The heart of Israel. Friday night.

Just a few hours before, my wife, Alyssa, and I had gotten off a very long international flight from New York. This was my first time in Israel. Before we left the States, our friends the Pryors, the ones who invited us and were already there, said, "Hey, meet us at this place in downtown Jerusalem when you land. If you can't find it, just ask the cab driver."

Our phones didn't work internationally, so we got into the cab at the airport with nothing but a name and a picture on our phone of a map. Surprisingly, it all worked out and we made it to the heart of Jerusalem, just a few blocks from Old Town.

Now, I'm not quite sure what I was expecting Israel and Jerusalem to look like—but sadly, due to no context, and too many sword-and-sandal Jesus-style movies, I was expecting the first century. But it was obviously the twenty-first, and we rolled into a hustling, bustling metropolis that didn't seem much different from a Manhattan side street or a Seattle thoroughfare—with obvious differences of language and culture.

We pulled up to the curb where our friends and mentors were waving us down. It's still surreal to think we successfully met up with them in another country at a specific place and time with no way to communicate during our travels. But we did it.

We walked up to their apartment with our huge bags in tow, then freshened up before joining them about an hour later for dinner.

It was a common, and normal, and actually very familiar scene at the restaurant:

Alyssa and I and a few other families—old, young, kids running around. There were plates of food, silverware, and all the normal signposts of the things we basically do at dinners every night of our lives. It seemed like a typical meal.

Then right when I was about to pick up my fork to start eating, the whole crew started singing and yelling (and hitting the table!) in unison, "*Shabbat shalom. Shabbat shalom. Shabbat shalom. Shabbat shabbat shabbat shabbaaaaatttt shalllllom.*"

I had no idea what they were doing, why they were doing it, and what they were saying, but within about .6 seconds I was trying to phonetically and loudly repeat their words. I was yelling, hitting the table, and I wanted *in*. All I knew was this felt very much like what I would call a party. You know that scene in *Dead Poet's Society* where all the students begin marching in circles in unison and they can't help it? I felt like that.

Then the fathers and mothers stood up and blessed their children. And not just the little kids but their teenage daughters and sons. And I mean *blessing*. There was standing involved, hands placed on heads, eye contact (awkward, right?), and more.

And what struck me the most was that the teenagers weren't recoiling. They weren't embarrassed. I was expecting the classic refrain, *"Daaaadddd, stopppppp"* as their father and mother placed their hands on their heads and blessed them with love. Scripture. Blessings.

And the real big game changer? We stayed there for almost a month—and this is what they did *every Friday night. It was expected.*

It all seemed so strange and different to me. Also, why were the teenagers even here? Wasn't Friday night the most valuable time of the week? Shouldn't they be out at the movies or downtown with their friends? And the more I thought about it, the more I realized that was true of everyone at the table, and I wondered how often, in our modern, Western downtown cities, we would find a few families over the size of twenty putting away all distractions and saying yes to each other for a feast and sacred meal every Friday night.

Let's back up and give the experience a little more context. We had some friends who lived in Jerusalem part time and had invited us to come stay with them to enjoy their company and friendships and the city and culture. They sent an email that started with, "If you're reading this, then that means we are . . . ," which is also eerily close to how I imagine most spy emails start, so I got excited.

And then we hopped on a plane.

Alyssa was five months pregnant with Kinsley, our first, so as new parents-to-be we were wide-eyed, with a mix of shock and horror and delight and expectancy in every situation we found ourselves in. We were on the lookout for how we would do this family thing.

As we walked around Israel during the next week, we saw things that were not common in the United States but seemed normal in Israel. Dads gathering at the park with their kids or pushing strollers down the street. Restaurants filled with families of seven or nine or twelve (grandparents, aunts, everyone included). Alyssa and I joked that in the US the restaurant limit at a table is four people. Two parents, two kids. If you have more than that and you try to come into a US establishment, you are a burden.

In Israel we routinely sat with other families at large tables, full of feasting and drinking and eating and laughing and songs. The grandparents seemed to *matter*. In fact, they were the ones leading or sitting at the head of many tables.

That first night in Israel, Alyssa and I realized just how special and rich and delightful it was to be there for a traditional shabbat dinner. It's like Christmas dinner, but it happens every Friday night. *Shabbat shalom.* After the eating and the blessings and hands put on the kids (things that just don't happen where I grew up), we hung out on our friends' balcony overlooking the Jerusalem skyline. I asked my friend Jeremy what had been on my mind all night: Why did families seem so radically different, and also stronger and happier, here?

Without missing a beat, Jeremy looked at me and said, "Individualism hasn't quite seeped in as strongly here, and they see the family as one of the main places to find an identity and the primary vehicle for bringing blessing and goodness into the world. In America, Christian or secular, we just simply don't believe that. Families are teams here, and the Scriptures are their playbook."

To which I felt confused and slightly defensive. Weren't the Scriptures our playbook too?

But then I realized he used the word *team*. That wasn't the first time I had heard him talk about family as a team, and it was starting to seem quite the X factor. That there was some secret sauce the Western, modern world had left out that more ancient cultures had been attuned to. That the hyper-individualism of our culture almost acted as a block to strong families and groups.

But let's take a little detour to a year before that, when the seed of questioning our presumptions about family was really planted.

Back in 2012, I had the strange privilege of having a video of me talking for four and a half minutes go viral. All of a sudden I had a lot of people wanting to talk to me, to get something from me or give something to me, or wanting me to give them advice—and I wasn't quite sure how to best steward that moment. I had just graduated from college and finished a church internship program, so my logical next step was to pursue a role in church, to be a pastor or something in that regard. But here was the problem: I inherently didn't feel cut out for that. It felt like fitting a square peg into a round hole. I wanted to create. Make things. Think outside the box. Carve a different path. Most of the advice I was getting, however, was to go on staff at a church. Become a pastor.

But my best friend said, "Hey, I know this guy named Jeremy Pryor who's a family friend, and he runs a successful online video company in Cincinnati and loves Jesus and has an awesome family. He's really creative and entrepreneurial, and I think it could be really illuminating to pick his brain for a few hours. Let me email him."

I lived in Washington state at the time and Jeremy lived in Ohio, so I figured we'd have a Skype call at best. But then Jeremy not only said yes, he said, "I'll come to you. I just booked a ticket for Thursday."

What was even more surprising, though, is he was the only—and I mean only—person who gave me advice that encouraged me in where I actually wanted to go. He said something different from everyone else. "This thing that happened to you was really special, and you should pay attention to why it happened and how you are uniquely wired to maybe keep doing the same thing—creatively using your gifts to start conversations about Jesus on the internet. Why would you stop that and do something else?"

When the meeting was over, for the first time I felt, *He's right, I could keep doing this.* I kept thinking about it over the next week, and that thought was making me feel alive.

About a week after the meeting, I walked to the mailbox and saw a letter from Jeremy. Inside was a check for $10,000, with a note: "I've thought about our meeting since we left last week. I believe in you and believe you have a peculiar and unique gift to keep doing this and I want to support you and where God is taking you. Go buy everything you need to level this up and make it something sustainable—cameras, lights, editing software, a working laptop if you need one, and anything else."

Not to be too vulnerable here, but my first thought was, *Is this what a true father is like?* because I didn't really know the answer to that question.

And it was not just about the money. I was struck by the affirmation. The investing spirit. The support. The belief.

First, that's a lot of money to anyone I know. But it was *insane to me.* I grew up on welfare and food stamps, and at that point I was twenty-two, living with ten other guys, sleeping on a homemade bunkbed, paying $200 a month rent (kind of a deal, I know!).

Just a few months before this moment, I had discovered an overdraft charge on my bank when I tried to buy some Peachie O's gummy candy and an AriZona Arnold Palmer iced tea (I think the total was $3.17), while filling up on gas. (Worth it by the way! Arnold Palmer is life.)

What I found even more striking was that Jeremy didn't ask for anything in return. He was just living generously, kingdom minded, and investing and following the Lord's Spirit and prompting. In fact, we didn't even talk after this! Life just moved on with his incredible investment and support of me. But two years later Alyssa and I found ourselves in a small town in Ohio. I was speaking at a conference in Harrison and remembered that Jeremy lived nearby.

It was delayed and long overdue, but we finally met up with Jeremy and his wife, April, at a Cracker Barrel (who knew you could get a nineteen-plate breakfast with every possible breakfast food known to man for six dollars? And those cheese grits!). If our first conversation changed my life from a vocational standpoint, this second one changed it from a family and marriage standpoint.

Have you ever had those conversations over a meal or with others where you feel like you're fully coming alive? It's so stimulating and intriguing and revelatory that you come away a different person? Something unlocks and clicks in a way that you can't unsee it? Yeah, this was that moment.

And it wasn't even like there was a specific purpose or goal to the conversation. We just started talking, and Alyssa and I kept peppering them with questions. As we asked them questions about their family and life in Cincinnati, everything coming out of their mouths sounded so strange and alluring and different. They even called themselves Team Pryor.

From their description we sensed the individuals of the family absolutely flourished, but it was obvious there was a collective DNA—a strong sense of "we are a unit for the kingdom of God" that I hadn't seen or experienced before. Their family seemed like a distinctly weird organism that was wildly different from any family I had ever heard of.

Our evening with them basically consisted of two hours of me interviewing an alien.

"So you own a bunch of businesses and real estate not because of money but because you see them as vehicles for the family team to work and do projects together?"

"What do you mean you *host and want and invite* the grandparents every week for a family game night? Isn't the goal to 'leave and cleave'?"

"You bought a duplex for your family to live in, just so you could use the other half to welcome families, single moms, friends in transition, and other people passing through and give them a soft spot to land because you believe the home is more central than most think?"

The feeling I had then, but can articulate much better now, is they were the first family I had ever known who seemed to truly believe the home was the main focus of activity— economically, spiritually, physically, and more. Family was the hub around which every other spoke turned, according to them. My idea of home at the time was a lot flimsier and weaker—home and family were for recharging to go back out into the world that truly mattered.

Their middle daughter was maybe nine at the time and was asking for opportunities to serve her friends in the neighborhood, so they were helping her craft a weekly group where she would invite her friends over for a structured time of teaching and encouragement.

They kept, in passing, talking about this "Family Meal" thing they'd do every Friday night that involved grandparents and storytelling and candles and songs that sounded like this deeply powerful (and weird) and ritual shaping of family identity.

They shared how their eleven-year-old daughter was finishing up writing her first book. How another kid had a few business ideas they were helping her with.

They mentioned different ministry or business opportunities, and I kept noticing how they would always say "we" instead of "I," making mention of how each kid (they have five) was fully activated within their giftings to work together and help that ministry or business opportunity.

For example, their two oldest kids, who were twelve and thirteen at the time, were currently in the middle of an experiment where the parents were allowing the kids to live on their own for a few weeks in a property next door that they owned as an "adult onboarding session." (Sadly, I know too many twenty-somethings who could use an "adult onboarding session," myself included.)

The kids had to pay rent, buy their own groceries, and feed themselves and didn't have any specific rules to follow nor did they have to be under the normal ones at home.

I was with their family not long after that and remember asking the two oldest about the experiment after it was over. And to hear the twelve-year-old boy say things like, "Yeah, it was awesome. I spent all our money on candy and stayed up until 3:00 a.m. the first few nights, but then I got sick and realized we had nothing to eat on day four, and it really taught me a lesson" was quite profound. Because the rest of the nation and their peers, myself included, usually learn that lesson square in the middle of college, when the stakes are much higher, and factors like alcohol make the decisions much dumber and costlier.

Then the oldest daughter began recounting how difficult it was to pay rent and get food and make decisions with her brother when the parents weren't there to help mediate when they reached an impasse.

But as I was sitting at that Cracker Barrel, I just kept thinking about and was dying to know why this family had radically shaped themselves to look so profoundly different from any family I had ever encountered.

So I asked him, and I still remember his exact response:

"Jeff, we aren't doing anything strange. Most Western families are the strange ones. God's idea, and we see this in so many ancient families, has always been multigenerational family teams on mission, and everything flows from that. The West just simply doesn't believe that, and it shows."

But with my background—and my definition of family growing up—what they were doing seemed *completely strange to me*. Family to me meant no dad present, a single mom, mental illness, and so much more.

———

Stable is where horses live. It certainly wasn't the home I grew up in.

I have a lot of fond memories of my childhood. My mom was a single mother who in many ways was superwoman. After becoming a parent myself, I realized I really don't know how she did it all. She was my biggest supporter, someone who made unbelievable sacrifices to catapult me out of the cycle of poverty and give me a fighting chance.

But I also have a lot of pretty hard childhood memories.

Of my mom getting so angry and having no way to control me as a boy, so the de facto punishment was pulling my ear so hard I thought it was literally going to rip off. This was sometimes a weekly occurrence.

Of leaving for middle school every morning and seeing my mom asleep in the living room. (I know now that is common for those suffering from depression and, as she learned later, being bipolar as well, and we lived in government-subsidized housing, so the living room was her bedroom.) When I'd come home from school, she'd still be sleeping in the living room.

Or that time she had an "episode" while my aunt was over, and the scene seemed to reflect a demon exorcism you see in movies.

Or the time I was staying at my dad's house for the weekend and we got a call in the middle of the night to come pick up my mom from jail because she had manically gone to my friend's house drunk and banged on the windows and doors, yelling incoherently, and they called the cops.

Things started to make a little more sense when my mom was diagnosed as bipolar when I got older. But it really wasn't until I was almost out of the house as a college student that there was stability, when she began to regularly take medication and seek help from mental health professionals.

And honestly, I don't fault my mom for any of this. Because, sadly, specifically in lower-income situations where scarcity reigns, patterns enmesh those living in them. There's no getting out. Poverty is a cycle and there are one thousand mini-deaths—death of not knowing, death of not knowing you don't know, death of lack of resources, death of lack of access, and more.

And so I was raised in chaos.

Sometimes my mom was in a good mood. Sometimes she was in a bad mood.

Reflecting on my childhood now, it's obvious how much the idea or concept of family had failed me. I'm not one of those millennials who blames my parents or upbringing for everything, but it's clear looking back on my life that the brokenness of the family structure and idea rained much pain, turmoil, and trauma on our life. And for those who know the childhood trauma literature, and the now popular ACE score (adverse childhood experience), I score a 5 or 6 (depending on how you count it) on the test, which puts me in the most risk-averse and generally most traumatized category (4 or more is seen as exceptionally high).

My whole life I always thought we were missing something by not being a "nuclear family." All throughout high school I was always hyperaware of how different many of my peers' and friends' families were from my own. Of course there were broken homes, and everyone had their own story to tell. But most of my friends in high school had two-parent, very well-off, stable families. And so at every playdate, every birthday party, and every graduation party, I was acutely reminded of just how my family and upbringing didn't look like theirs.

Theirs was a success. Mine wasn't. Theirs was what a family "should" look like. Or so I thought.

But now, a decade past that time, as I reflect on those relationships, the fruit doesn't seem as promising as I had hoped. Just within the landscape of my immediate peers from high school, there are stories of suicide, cocaine use, divorce, lack of purpose, depression. All before the age of thirty. And most of them came from stable and safe environments. What happened?

Now, there is absolutely no way to foolproof our lives from difficulty—that's not what I'm saying. No matter how we live (were raised or raise our kids) there will be enormous bumps and suffering and trials and pain and hurt. That is inevitable. I'm not talking about that. But the pattern does seem to emerge that it's nearly a pipe dream and impossible to imagine a healthy family that lasts more than one generation in our culture. It's a unicorn. Why is that?

There are a few explanations.

The first is that we haven't even acknowledged we are living in an experiment. And I call it an experiment for a reason. Across religions and cultures, the way we have operated and continually set up the family the last 150 to 200 years as a springboard only for the individual success of each person is a wild departure from how the family used to operate. We have been in an experiment of great proportions.

What is an experiment? The dictionary defines it in simple terms: the process of testing a hypothesis.

But just like I learned in middle school science class, what do you do at the end of an experiment? You examine the data and make conclusions. So when can we call it quits on the experiment? When can we actually examine the data to see if we want to keep going in that direction? Take just one area of how this has radically reshaped the family—fatherlessness:

- 24.7 million kids currently in America do not live with their biological father.[1]

TAKE BACK YOUR FAMILY

- Children are four times more likely to grow up in poverty if the father is not around.[2]
- Children without fathers in the home are more likely to have behavior problems, abuse drugs and alcohol, and on and on.

Those statistics are no surprise. There's a lot of different ways to look like a family team—but it's clear most teams are being blown up left and right in our culture. In fact, I tick every one of those boxes. But there is a strange moment in our culture right now where instead of simply being sad about the reality, we jump first to "I can do it without them, and I won't let that define me." Which is true. It shouldn't define us—but it's also okay to simply let it make us sad. And we can be sad and also admit there are situations where the father should not be present, like if he is abusive.

I'm not saying everything should be shoved back into some fake reality; in fact, there are a lot of different ways to be and look like a team! I'm just saying, *Don't we have a deep sense that this is not how it's supposed to be?*

And let's be honest—the deadbeat dad is the easy target. We admit that. We know that. But the failed experiment has permeated all areas.

Take the classic nuclear family.

Did you know America is by definition and according to statistics one of the worst places to raise a family in the developed world?

In the article "The Best Countries to Raise a Family in 2020," researchers looked at thirty-five of the world's developed countries and analyzed six factors along the lines of safety, happiness, cost, education, time, and health. They then ranked them and gave a typical school system score to each.

And only two countries of the thirty-five were given an F.

The United States and Mexico.

The USA. The land of the free and home of the brave. The place where "all your dreams can come true." And on every single metric we were at the bottom.

Families in the US are less educated, spend less time with their kids (Americans are born workaholics, are we not?), are less safe, and have less money. In every category America is one of the costliest places to have children.[3]

In fact, the study was so shocking and revealing about the true nature of family in the US that one researcher (raised in the USA and a parent herself) actually ran the numbers again. When she realized they were "undeniably correct," she chose to add an entire section qualifying the low scores: "Since the United States was in many ways an outlier, we felt it was necessary to give additional commentary, context and statistics on why the US ranked second to last on our list."[4]

Since the US earned an F in the categories of time and safety, she pointed out that it lacks the paid leave other countries offer, and its high numbers of homicides and shootings, along with deficiencies in human rights, have had negative long-term effects. Landing dead last in the cost category, she also noted that Americans spend over three times as much to deliver a baby than citizens of other countries, and then we spend 23 percent of our annual household income on childcare. Our families are not safe. We have no time for each other. We are unhappy. And unhealthy. That's what the data shows.

And that whole multigenerational thing? I think the silent killer is what our families are doing to our elderly. We in the West invented an entire industry—called nursing homes—to do what most people in history did within their own family.

We don't like to say it, but to us, elderly people are dispensable. We don't actually *need them* like cultures did in the past. Before, they were the gatekeepers, the sources of winsome and sage advice that had been hard fought for and hard won over decades of life experience. Now you can just google the answer, so why would you need your grandparents?

And this mindset is devastating both on an emotional and on a practical level.

First, emotionally, a recent study found that most elderly people in the UK go an entire week without having one conversation with another human![5] Who knew that the next time a guard at a prison wants to give an inmate solitary confinement he could just send them out into Western society.

And then many places like Japan and others are paying people to have more children, because they are finding that there are not enough people to take care of the elderly and the state simply can't do it by itself without imploding financially.[6]

I love how the psalmist reflects on this same truth, noting

in Psalm 68:6 that YHWH "sets the lonely in families." Not nursing homes. Not in front of a screen. Not among their peers. The place God has for lonely and isolated people? A family—and that can be actual family, or if we've been failed there, it can be an adoptive family or the church family. But a place of multigenerational diversity committed to one another and a place to rest and be known.

———

The nuclear family ideal is an experiment that absolutely needs to be declared bankrupt. It's failing, and it's over.

But let's reflect on the very specific truths of the experiment. The Western family ideal operates on two universal laws, spoken or otherwise assumed:

1. I am (or my success, feelings, and trajectory are) the most important thing, not my family. Essentially, I am *more important* than the family.
2. Anything that imposes limits on me, at my expense, is inherently wrong.

And while Western families are not printing out these two laws, framing them, and pledging allegiance to them every morning at breakfast, the contagion in the air subtly has infected us all. Like gravity, it's invisible, and we don't think about it too much, but it's all around us and affects us greatly.

FAMILY SPOTLIGHT

The Stone Family

QUIT EVERYTHING. TRUST GOD.

If God told you to quit your job and walk away from everything you've built, would you?

If you had kids, a wife, medical insurance, would you?

If your reason for doing so was nothing more than "God told me, and we will trust him," would you?

I probably wouldn't be able to, as much as I wish I had that kind of faith.

But that's exactly what the Stone family did. When the family team idea started taking root, it began to reorient everything they did as a family. And one main thing it began to touch was work and vocation and rest.

And that's when the sabbath year, or Shmita, started to get a little louder in the family's story.

In the Bible, this is a year that God commands his people to rest. To let the land have a break. It was actually a sustainability tactic—it was God's way of saying, "If you constantly work the land and don't let it rest, you will run it dry." (Sound like any of our lives?)

So Jordan and his family took the leap, even though he had a well-paying, stable leadership position as the manager of a Starbucks location.

Jordan said, "One of the first real crisis moments, even starting that first day after I quit as manager of Starbucks, was how obsessed I was with short-term returns and how much I realized my identity was in work. And I realized with parenting, there aren't that many short-term results. Parenting is a long-term play, and the year off taught me that more than anything.

"I thought the Christian dad's job was to 'provide for my family,' but really saw that solely through money.

"I remember reading about the sabbath years ago, and just kind of wondering why they didn't actually obey that and why no one does that today. Oh yeah, because it's *terrifying and scary.*

"So we decided to take God literally, and asked what it would look like if I took a year off from 'providing' for my family, to then return to provide for my family. What kind of year would we craft if it was fully devoted to providing for my family in all the ways I had overlooked years prior? So my wife and I got out some paper and started scribbling down why it would be a good idea and all the amazing things we would do for our family. And then we scribbled why it was a bad idea and we shouldn't. And as I looked at the 'shouldn't do it' list, I noticed every single one was based in fear.

"What about money? What about career advancement? What if I can't come back to this job?"

But that's the point—trusting God where it actually counts.

And spoiler alert: God took care of them. In more ways than they ever could have imagined.

The sabbath year is a reset. And they needed a complete family reset. So they decided to trust God.

"If God would have given us a full picture of that year before we did it, I probably wouldn't have done it. He intrigued us through needing rest and a reset, which we got even more than we thought. But one thing we didn't anticipate was there was all types of junk in our lives and marriage and in me that had been essentially suppressed through busyness and came roaring back during that year.

"Anything that is a priority should make a way onto your schedule, so we began with that and went from there.

"And then we found out we were pregnant two days after I quit. To me, that was a sign God was in it. If we had found out two days before I'd quit, I'm not sure I would've taken the jump—I needed health insurance and more."

Their choice transformed their life and marriage. It forced them to deal with the junk that was in the way of the closeness of their family. They had time to work on multi-generational bonds.

The Shmita is fascinating, as the principle states that you let the ground lie fallow; you eat what comes up, and they were eating the fruit of goodness that came up that year that God provided.

It's clear that the point of the year off in the Torah was for *healing and reset*. Not saying that we all need to take a year off, but has your family ever had even a season? Of rest and stoppage and resetting and healing? Or is the soil the same as our family and heart—dry, crusty, and overrun.

Jordan said, "During that year my heart came home. I learned that what I've got here (in my family) is the best thing I have going—and the most strategic. And the year off taught me that."

The big impact of Jordan's story is that we sometimes underestimate how a radical decision can help deepen our identity. We can believe "that's good for *their* family." (And it is.) But we don't think we need to do it, so we miss out on discovering how radical, sacrificial decisions actually help foster a family identity like nothing else can.

And it reminds me of the biblical story in the Torah when Moses reminded the Israelites of the importance of their choices: "when your children's children ask what happened that day" (Ex. 12:26, my paraphrase).

Because when we make radical decisions of faith, we actually have an answer to that question.

TWO

The Myth of the Nuclear Family

The nuclear family is the cancer, not the cure.

Nothing has done more damage to Scripture's vision of family than the ideal of the nuclear family.

What is the nuclear family? It's a concept of family that peaked in the 1950s and '60s that consisted of a mom, a dad, and two kids as the social unit. It generally centers itself on consumption, safety, and individual happiness. In other words, if we can get what we want, have nothing go wrong, and everyone does what he or she wants to do, then the family has done its job.

But the interesting thing about this nuclear family ideal is that it's a myth, a unicorn, and a flat-out bad idea. It's based on the 1950s family, when the conditions of an unprecedented postwar prosperity (one of the greatest booms in our history) led to a fifteen-year lightning strike, a golden period of stability and achievability, but that version of the nuclear family will never make a return. The nuclear family is more fragile than a china plate, which is why it only lasted for fifteen years.

Those who most advocate for the nuclear family, Christians, don't seem to want to return to a biblical vision in any sense of the word. They are not chasing an ancient picture of family. They are chasing 1950; they just want *Leave It to Beaver.*

But the 1950s family is in many ways antithetical to the Scriptures—not least in the fact that it was based on consumption, while the first-century family was based on production. The ancient picture of family was a robust, intergenerational, complex, and enormously helpful web of relationships where the most vulnerable and downtrodden were welcomed, protected, and given a safety net.

Some have responded to the 1950s vision with a call for a wider definition of family. As David Brooks noted in his seminal article "The Nuclear Family Was a Mistake," "People should have the freedom to pick whatever family form works for them," while completely shutting their eyes to the mountainous data that suggests the obvious truth that certain family forms simply do not work well for a lot of people.

"In other words, while social conservatives have a philosophy of family life they can't operationalize, because it no longer is relevant, progressives have no philosophy of family life at all, because they don't want to seem judgmental. The sexual revolution has come and gone, and it's left us with no governing norms of family life, no guiding values, no articulated ideals. On this most central issue, our shared culture often has nothing relevant to say—and so for decades things have been falling apart."[1]

The more conservative people among us say, "Let's bring back the power of the family!" But the vision is an actual impossibility for everyone except the rich, and not a true historical or biblical vision of family anyway.

The more liberal folks among us say, "The family doesn't matter. Do what you want. Family is anyone and everyone, right?"

Both are wrong (with both also holding a sliver of truth, like usual).

One of the worst and most insidious parts of our vision of the nuclear family is it only widens the gap between the haves and the have-nots. As Brooks said, "The shift from bigger and interconnected extended families to smaller and detached nuclear families ultimately led to a familial system that liberates the rich and ravages the working-class and the poor."

Basically, what Brooks argued is that we cannot survive without extended or "corporate family," but in our society today, the rich can buy that extended family by hiring nannies, caretakers, tutors, and more.

And so we have demanded our individual freedom. At all costs. Removing all institutional safeguarding for our own self leads to the very destruction and slavery we think we are getting away from. But in an ideal everyone can aspire to, only the wealthy can actually achieve it. What more unjust system than a picture of family that is only possible *when you can buy it*? One easy litmus test for God's vision for the world is, if it's worse for the poor, it's most likely not his vision.

According to our collective wisdom, we are not free until we need no one, rely on no one, and depend on nothing. A recent *Rolling Stone* article said it even better: "The American cult of the individual denies not just community but the very idea of society. No one owes anything to anyone. All must be prepared to fight for everything: education, shelter, food, medical care."[2]

But is that freedom or slavery? I'd argue the latter. Making us now slaves to machines. Slaves to lack of love. Slaves to ourselves.

A world of wage stagnation, rising living costs, and the need for both parents to work simply out of necessity is the norm in our current culture. The Western ideal is a luxury. And the last time I checked, for something to be really true it needs to be true and possible for all.

We graduate college with tens of thousands of dollars in debt, now needing a job just to keep the bank from coming after us. (Few of us pick vocations or jobs now based on purpose but instead on what will help us pay our loans back the quickest.) But one job isn't enough by any means to make it in most places, so both spouses are now working as hard as they can just to keep their heads above water.

Then they start having kids. Now who's going to take care of the baby? We both have to work or we won't have enough money to survive and live and pay our bills. And the United States has some of the worst paternity and maternity leave policies in the entire world, so you will have to choose between the enormously difficult decision of quitting your job or only taking a brief time off while you just welcomed a new life into the world. If you do think about quitting, you will have to wrestle with the fact that you may not find employment again after taking years off when your children are small and will be harshly penalized in wage and status if you try to resume your career ten years later.

Or you decide not to quit and put your child in daycare, with the higher-end states averaging (yes, averaging, which means many go above this) around $2,500 per month for childcare.[3] But one of you only makes about $50k per year, since middle-class wages have completely stagnated, yet cost of living has skyrocketed.[4] And so you use more than half of your entire salary to have someone else watch your kids so you can work to use more than half of that salary to have someone watch your kids. The cycle is vicious . . . yet somehow normal, since a lot of us are doing it.

Oh, and the leftover money? That's used for the crazy student debt you incurred to get a degree to become more "employable," since student education costs have far outpaced any other cost over the last few decades. And those necessary things like food, shelter, rent, clothing, savings, emergency fund, and others? Well, let's hope you have a few dollars to cover those things too.

And by the way, that's the current situation of the "normative" married two-parent household. Don't get me started on the insurmountable mountain of difficulty that parents of special-needs children and single parents face in our current system.

My single mom had to work multiple jobs to keep us out of dire poverty and just above homelessness (all while attempting to get a college degree in night school at the local community college). And this was even though we were in government-subsidized housing for my entire life, I had lunch provided by the state through the school system for more than a decade, and our groceries were paid for with food stamps.

All this to say, our systems and pictures and relationships and visions of what a family is and what it means and what it's supposed to do are flatly broken. Yet we must first acknowledge we are simply living the logical conclusion of where this wave was taking us in the first place—from the Enlightenment (the unhindered and unrestrained individual is the most important pursuit), to the Industrial Revolution (the complete disintegration of vocation and family and the transfer of the economic center from the household to the factory), to the nuclear family being an impossible ideal to aspire to (when in reality it was just a little bit of unprecedented growth and prosperity post-WWII that even made it work in the first place).

———

When Alyssa was pregnant with our first child, I began to wrestle with the idea of family. I felt like there was so much untangling to do. The spirit of individualism and the spirit of family as homes of consumption ran so deep, was so ingrained, and flowed throughout every fiber of our Western existence.

Most of us can easily recall or trace harsh memories or brokenness specifically with family that has caused us to feel like we have been failed by the system of family.

There is probably a very obvious reason the modern family has failed you.

1. Your parents divorced when you were a kid, and you were left to pick up the pieces.

2. You were raised in a fundamentalist religious family that centered on shame and guilt, not on life and flourishing.

3. Porn (or addiction) led to devastating consequences in your family.

4. The pressure of performance and how your family looked—athletically, morally, and in school—took precedence over your soul as it withered over the years in isolation and mask wearing.

5. Or—my story—you were raised by a single mom who is a superhero, because your parents never were together

for that long or never got married and your dad didn't want to be that involved.

I could go on and on naming hypotheticals, but the truth is most people fit into at least one of those scenarios.

I felt like the actual way we lived as a family was eating our very family. It just didn't feel right. I needed a detox. A better story. A different image.

Around that same time I was doing a ton of research for my book *To Hell with the Hustle*, which is about our culture's view of work and production and identity formation. And I was reading a lot about the Industrial Revolution specifically, the birth of large-scale behemoth factories and the assembly line, and just how insidious that particular moment was in our country's shaping of work and family.

And that's when it struck me. The factory (and all its detriments) is an enormous metaphor for the Western family. Western families *are* factories. How? Factories are monstrosities of the Gilded Age, a time of immense economic growth in the late nineteenth century, and their job was to extract the highest value at the most efficient rate and lowest cost. Take as much as you can, produce as much as you can, consume as much as you can, and do it as quickly as you can before you shut down. (Have you ever noticed how most factories close within a generation or two? They aren't built to last; they are built to extract and die.) And our families are the same—use each other and the household to extract as many things, entertainments, and personal goals as we can before the family self-destructs.

As writer Wendell Berry put it:

> Marriage, in other words, has now taken the form of divorce: a prolonged and impassioned negotiation as to how things shall be divided. During their understandably temporary association, the "married" couple will typically consume a large quantity of merchandise and a large portion of each other.
>
> The modern household is the place where the consumptive couple do their consuming. Nothing productive is done there. Such work as is done there is done at the expense of the resident couple or family, and to the profit of suppliers of energy and household technology. For entertainment, the inmates consume television or purchase other consumable diversion elsewhere.[5]

So marriage in America now is only a metaphor for divorce—compete against each other and grab what you can as you negotiate how things should be consumed. *Consume things, until you consume each other.*

I started asking, what is the opposite of a factory? There has to be a better way, right?

And I realized, our concept of a farm (before they were radically industrialized) holds a lot of the powers that the factory loses. And so let's ask ourselves, is our family factory

TAKE BACK YOUR FAMILY

formed or farm formed? One leads to life; the other leads to
death. Here's how I've been processing it:

FACTORY FORMED	FARM FORMED
Centers around consumption	Centers around contribution
Acts like a club	Looks like a team
Linear with no limits	Rhythmic and lives within limits
Outsource	Ownership
Amnesia	Story formed

Also note the characteristic of speed: a factory creates
something overnight, while farms take months or years of
work before you see much fruit. In our families so many of us
are wanting and demanding quick results. (All we are doing
is showing our cards. We really do think we are factories
anyway.)

One of the biggest changes around the time of industrialization was the large-scale moving of economic activity
around work to a new location. Before, say, 1800, most of the
buzz and hub was located within the household. The household was the headquarters, the room in *Hunger Games* where
the gamemaker could see everything and move all the pieces.
Most (again, generalizing here) families were self-sustaining
businesses and units. It was an agrarian- and trade-dominated
society, where most people worked the land, owned a farm,
were bread makers for the past eight generations, and so on.

The dad wasn't a bread maker. The family was a family of

bread makers. It was a team unit. I actually find it somewhat comical that some conservatives want to return to the "good ol' days" when moms stayed home and took care of the kids and babies—because those weren't the good ol' days. That change was a weird disruption of work and home that happened as recently as the Industrial Revolution.

For most of human history, the reality was moms stayed home because the business was at home. Husband and wife were the executive leadership team and board of directors. They were both running the well-oiled machine of the family farm or the trade. Moms were bosses and "doing it all" long before it was cool and the #girlboss movement existed, and they were doing it in a household, as part of the family team, rather than the shallow interpretation of competing interests where one must win and one must lose (family versus work life).

Now, the obvious question becomes, Jeff, are you saying we all just need to work from home? No, not at all. I'm saying we need to reimagine what it's like to center the household as a place of identity and production—whether we work from there or not.

The magic before industrialization was not simply that everyone was together and everyone was home; it was that life was integrated. Dads worked *in front of their kids*. Taught their kids their craft that they'd honed and cultivated over the years. They passed it on. They discipled with their life.

Then all of a sudden, factories started opening, production

boomed, and now mindless workers were needed. By the droves. And in a flash, we had a country where Dad gets up and leaves for work in the morning and spends most of his time away from his family and with a different team. Robert Bly's book *Iron John* traces this phenomenon: the kids in this parable don't know what their parents do for work, much less understand it, and it affects the parent/child relationship. The disconnect is vast.

Somehow this new factory life gets painted as the ideal of success for the wholesome family that we see in ads from the 1950s and movies like *Pleasantville.* The "Honey, I'm home!" type of life. Does anyone else see something wrong with this? Factories are about divide and conquer. Efficiency. Specialization.

No wonder most moms are drowning and sinking and overwhelmed. Our model created that. For mass efficiency and lowest friction.

So dads left and started working in factories, and it had immense ramifications. A family was no longer a unit or a team. It was a group of individuals all pursuing their own interests or goals and then collecting resources, coming home, and sharing those resources.

And what's crazy is that sometimes our answers to the problem are backward. What did we come up with as a solution? Not bring the dad home. But send the mom out to work too!

More *disintegration.*

What if the answer to the disorder we are feeling isn't

more working moms but more integrated households? This is why I never really know how to answer the question when someone asks me if I am a feminist.

Like most complex questions, I usually respond by asking, "What do you mean by feminist?" If by feminism you mean equality of man and woman, with that entire half of the gender flourishing and living in freedom and living fully into themselves as image bearers of God, then yes, I'm a feminist. And I'd say it's obvious Jesus is too.

But if you mean a reductionist view that women need to leave the house and go work more out of the home, then that's a train I can't necessarily jump on. And let's make sure we all heard what I wrote a few paragraphs above. I think saying the same thing about dads is a train I can't jump on either, even though that ship has sailed, and that train has been running, and getting faster and faster, for a long time.

In some ways, feminism is basically seeing the entire fabric of work and disintegration of craft and sacredness of our labor over the past hundred years and saying, "Hey, I want in on that too!"

What I'm saying is we need to jump ship—both men and women. We've created a monster of a culture, and we can't all just wake up one day and own a family farm or start a family business, nor do all of us want to, but have we even given our choices a second thought?

We might say it's necessary for both parents to work outside the home. But have we ever pushed back on our own idea of necessary? What's necessary? To have a certain size home? To make enough money so we can spend it on entertainment and consumption? What have we actually produced with our work and life? Will we be proud in twenty years with our life's body of work?

Now, for the sake of being as clear as absolutely possible, I want to repeat: I am in no way, shape, or form saying the solution is just to work at home. That is a caricature. And we all did that during COVID, didn't we? And our families didn't magically change overnight (though the brief period of work stoppage has been a hidden blessing to many even despite the difficulties). What I'm saying is our culture has created a culture of disintegration. We are getting further and further apart. Our family box doesn't touch our work box, and neither of those touch our hobby box. What I'm saying is my "father-ness" should go with me everywhere. And sometimes I leave and go and work, but I do not lose my father identity in those moments—and that is one small way of being integrated.

The nuclear family is the locker room of disintegration, individualism, and consumption. Just ask Carle Zimmerman, a social scientist at Harvard University who was arguably one of the more powerful and well-respected and well-known social scientists in all of academia from the 1920s to the 1940s. He was a giant in the field of family research during his life-time, and he ran seriously counter to the main thrust of other academics at the time.

Popular during this time, the Chicago school of thought

founded by Ogburn and Folsom, which focused on the fact that the family under industrialization had essentially been castrated and was only a "parking place" for parents and children, since their active hours of production and meaning were now found elsewhere. But this was good change, they believed. It was also inevitable, and they thought we as a society should accelerate the process as fast as we can.

They believed that "mothers should be mobilized for full-time employment, small children should be put into collective day care, and other measures should be adopted to effect 'the individualization of the members of society.'"[6] Their words, not mine. And this was in the '40s, by the way—almost a century ago.

Zimmerman had no disagreements with the indictment of the nuclear family as a parking place that gives members safety but no identity, since identity is usually found in what we produce or where we are most productive—aka the workplace for the parent, school for the kid. (Note: Is home a place you "park" your family, or does it feel like the buzzing hotbed of mission and identity for the rest of life it should be?) Zimmerman believed the problem wasn't the family itself, but rather the model it took on.

Zimmerman's *Family and Civilization* was his lasting response to this issue that was just beginning to show itself in modern America. He didn't use the word *nuclear* like we do, but instead used the phrase "atomistic family" to essentially mean the same thing (the phrase *nuclear family* wasn't popular until after he died). He said the atomistic family is not a vision of the peak healthy society. In fact, he argued that when the atomistic family shows up in a society, it actually is a sign that that culture is close to collapse.

Yes, you read that right.

Now, if that's not counter to all the arguments from conservative groups right now, I don't know what is.

Zimmerman specifically studied the rise and fall of major empires throughout history, such as the Greeks and Romans, and noted very particular patterns of what families look like during the height and decline of civilizations. He found across eras there are generally three different stages of families that tend to live at different times and mean different things in the story of that civilization:

- the trustee family,
- the domestic family, and
- the atomistic family.

These three, he argued, go in succession toward decline. Meaning no strong civilization has ever been built that didn't have powerful trustee families. (He even showed that every change of power between empires is almost always a trustee family–based society defeating an atomistic family society.) That is the thing that usually builds an empire or a global power. And most have declined and faded away once the predominant model becomes atomistic.

Now, let's break this down a little with definitions of these terms.

The trustee family is where the living members are not the entirety of the family but are merely "trustees" of its blood, rights, property name, and position for their lifetime. It's not the nuclear family, or even the extended family, but "all the members of the family in the past and the future as well as in the present generation."[7] A sacred bond unites members in the present generation with the ancestors who gave them life; the same bond unites them with their future descendants, who will perpetuate the family name. A good way to think about it is, the family is whoever has had that last name in all the historical line (including all the maiden names that were merged). Think the Capulets and Montagues in *Romeo and Juliet*.

In trustee familial societies, the family is virtually where all power is held, not government or other civic institutions. While I'd prefer not to go back to medieval times with fiefdoms and land wars, and actually think this model has some exceptionally large cons about it (loss of individual, the weakest members are usually lost or left in the dust, which is anti-biblical), there are things we can learn from this, while also seeing the spirit of trustee families alive and well in the West in a more business or political way rather than the way of the fifteenth century.

If I say the Kennedys or the Rockefellers to you, you will almost surely know who I'm talking about, and that is obvious fruit of a trustee family in a nuclear society—legacies and last names that are passed down generationally to mean something. (What pains me about many large, looming American families is how corroded and harmful they can become when they are not saturated in a biblical ethic of love and self-sacrifice.)

Then there is the domestic family. "The domestic family describes a household based on the marital bond: husband, wife and their children. In such an arrangement, family members emphasize individual rights along with family duties."[8]

Essentially, the family and marital unit are a team and hold a strong identity without losing individuality and purpose. The domestic family is just the right balance where family is larger than the individual yet not crushing to the individual. And guess what? Zimmerman noted in his research that it's not a coincidence that most societies at their peak creativity and power are almost always in a state of domestic families being strong.

In his own words, domestic families "possess a certain amount of mobility and freedom and still keep up the minimum amount of familism necessary for carrying on the society." He even noted the striking difference between cities and rural areas when he was writing (1947), with there almost being a gap between rural areas still showing domestic families while cities were bending atomistic.

Then there is the atomistic family, which is defined when "individual rights are exalted far above family bonds, and the family itself exists for the sake of the individual's pleasure."[9] Or, as he put it another place, the "unrestrained individual" is the chief aim or purpose of living, and family is both an impediment and an agent to use to that gain. And the minute a society goes "atomistic" is the minute individualism becomes cancerous.[10]

The advertisements, the radio, the movies, housing construction, leasing of apartments, jobs—everything is individualized. The advertisers depict and appeal to the fashionably small family. In the motion pictures, the family seems to be motivated by little more than self-love. Dining rooms are reduced in size. Children's toys are cheaply made; they seldom last through the interest period of one child, much less several. The whole system is *un-familistic*.

Zimmerman argued the elites who are centered in cities are usually the first domino to fall. As they go, so does everyone else. If they don't believe or care about family, soon enough no one will because they have all the power and begin to form institutions in their own image—ones that center only on the individual, unhindered freedom, and endless choices of pleasure.

And his prediction couldn't have been any more on the nose. In the *Atlantic*, Derek Thompson noted how cities have essentially become an "Epcot theme park for childless affluence, where the rich can act like kids without having to actually see any."[11]

And this is not a religious soapbox, using pro-family arguments to suit my case-type of moment. Zimmerman was nonreligious and simply was looking at the data and the research. Countries are finally starting to pay attention—places like Japan and Hungary and others are literally paying people to have children. Why? Not because they love children, but because they are seeing it to be absolutely devastating to their economy if they don't. In short, if countries were businesses, lack of domestic strong families is putting them on the verge of bankruptcy. But it might be too late. In Hungary enormous tax breaks and housing benefits are given to couples who have children, yet the fertility rate is still drastically low and well below the replacement rate (the scientific rate of making sure enough people are born to take care of the previous generation).[12] Thompson noted that "might suggest that couples in advanced economies—and, in particularly, educated mothers in advanced economies—simply don't want more children."

But Zimmerman had called it. In 1947. Just before the nuclear family golden era of 1950 to 1970, as David Brooks noted. And if we had been listening or paying attention, we would have realized it wasn't a golden era at all, but the last domino falling.

As John Paul II so eloquently said back in 1981, "The future of humanity passes by way of the family."[13]

We first have to go after the problems—individualism, industrialization, and more—before we can chat about the blueprint and ways to turn the ship. And how being a strong family team can counteract all those negative currents we are so mindlessly floating down the river of destruction on.

But I have good news too—and that is every family can be a team, not just the ideal sometimes talked about by Christian preachers of the two-parent, suburb-living, soccer-playing, homeschooling family. The ideal is not two parents, two kids, one dog; the ideal is a multigenerational family team on mission (and that doesn't even have to mean a family by blood). And I want to say that everyone—no matter the life stage or age—can take a step in that direction. And more steps for the next one hundred years. Because that's how long it takes to build something that big.

Single parents
Blended families
Divorced spouses
Special-needs families
Two-parent families
Chronic-illness families
Adoptive or foster-parent families

And I'm sure there are even more differences and unique circumstances I could name, but those are ones off the top of my head. And how do I know it's possible no matter the stage or type of family? Because we see it every month in our Homeroom program at Family Teams (an online community of a few thousand families trying to live this out together and share ideas, and so forth). Homeroom is an online group centered around a specific tool meant to help family teams (like naming your team, creating rituals, and understanding a mission), and it includes people from all across the nation—and it blesses and encourages me every single day. The "Family Spotlight" sections in this book highlight families from our Homeroom group. I'm thinking of them and you all as I write this book.

God has a wild vision for your family that is near, if we would reach out and touch it. He has a vision so big for your family that it will outlast you and outlive you. His blessing on you will pass on to a thousand generations. And he will make his face shine upon you and give you peace.

THREE

Sears Shaped How We Think About Family

Imagine you live in Ohio, Illinois, or Pennsylvania, and you're out for a walk with your dog. Across the street is a group of people with clipboards, shuffling some catalog of sorts and holding a few cameras. They stop every few houses and size it up as they look at their clipboard and catalog.

You aren't sure what they are doing, but you shrug it off, since they seem harmless. As you're finishing your walk and heading back up your stairs to enter the house, you hear them coming behind you.

"Hi, ma'am. Can we come look in your basement for a minute?"

And let's say for cordiality's sake you entertain them. "Um. What are you looking for in my basement?"

"We are looking for the number D655. We hope to find it in a few pieces of lumber in your basement."

This would be almost identical to encounters people had with the real-life group, the Kit House Hunters.

In the late 1990s, Rebecca Hunter picked up an old Sears catalog and took a walk around the neighborhood. In the catalog she noticed that there were kit homes being advertised in the early twentieth century.

"For $945 you can build an eight-room bungalow style house!" (This was an advertisement from Sears' first kit home, sold in 1908.)[1]

The mail-order homes from Sears were the logical conclusion to Sears & Roebuck's incredibly popular mail catalog. This was the Amazon before Amazon. In the first decade of the century, one-fifth of Americans had this catalog sitting on their coffee table or nightstand. It offered more than a hundred thousand items and got to be fourteen hundred pages long and weighed four pounds! The best part? It was free, because Sears knew they made their money by getting you to see all you could order.

And so in 1908, Sears decided to ship entire homes to people for them to build themselves. They were DIY long before Pinterest.

They made it as frictionless as possible. You'd see your desired floor plan and home design in the catalog, place an order, send in a check, and a few weeks later a train car would roll in just for you. The door hatch of the train car even had a small wax seal you would break to ensure you were the first to open it. Inside you'd find more than ten thousand pieces of lumber, twenty thousand cedar shakes, all the way down to the screws, bolts, doors, doorknobs, and more. Oh, and a seventy-five-page manual with instructions. Everything was precut and ready to be screwed, nailed, or framed together.

Sears promised you could do it without a carpenter—only basic skills required—and it would most likely take you less than ninety days. They ended up shipping more than seventy-five thousand homes in just thirty years. And in doing so they changed the entire landscape of housing on many fronts, from ushering out custom homes to making homes affordable and more standardized.

This is why homes around one hundred years old or older are usually more opulent, detailed, complex, and "one of a kind," and ones after aren't. Sears began the trend of factory-stamped and standardized houses. And then you'd have a brand-new empty home just waiting to be filled with stuff. And where could you get everything you needed to fill that empty home?

Sears.

Around the middle of the century, the program closed and the trend was over and had been all but forgotten until a fateful cold day when Rebecca Hunter took a walk with this catalog for no reason other than intrigue and began to inspect homes in her neighborhood and compare the pictures she'd see in the catalog. In Elgin, Illinois, where she was walking, she found an exact match within minutes.

And that walk has now turned into an enormous blog and website called Kit House Hunters, which has identified more than fifty thousand Sears Kit Homes around the nation—with the verifying parts numbers on beams found in the basement (stamped, for example, with D655) or with an address found on those beams, or 925 Homan Avenue, which was Sears headquarters at the time.

But Sears home kits didn't only change the landscape of housing in America by standardizing and industrializing it. They also had an even bigger but more subtle and pervasive effect—they kickstarted the radical shift of multigenerational living to single family homes.

Before Sears homes, most families in America lived multigenerationally—usually three generations, if not more, lived together, sometimes with peer-level cousin families or an uncle and aunt in the mix as well. The homes were sprawling (not just bigger, but with wings of the home). In fact, this is still how most of the world lives in one form or another. Having spent time in a place like Israel, the contrast is stark. During our trip to Israel, we thought the large buildings we saw were condos or apartment buildings; they were actually multigenerational dwellings.

But Sears needed more customers back in the day, and what is the most genius way to get more customers? Create them! Create a need for something that didn't exist.

Most families in their current multigenerational dwelling already had a house and liked it. But soon teenagers would grow up to become young adults and get married. And that was a ripe opportunity.

As one research source on the topic noted: "Sears looked at this idyllic scene of [multigenerational] families living in harmony and saw . . . a wasted opportunity. Why should newly-weds move into old homes filled with old things when they could move into new homes and fill them with new things from Sears?"[2]

And just like that, the twentieth-century version of Amazon was not the only factor but was one of the strongest foundational factors that split apart generational living and helped "kickstart single family living."[3]

I'm not going to argue that everyone should live with or near their parents. For some of you reading this, that is a *bad idea*. But what I am saying is that we are more fragmented and disintegrated generationally than we have ever been in all human history. And that's a problem.

Eric Weinstein, a famed mathematician and economist, had a salient point about this in an interview I listened to recently. He noted that essentially the middle half of the century was a mass scale shift: "people moved away from family support systems and toward financial support systems."[4] Because of the postwar economic boom, and the creation of the middle class, it was the first time many people could afford not to live by or with their parents or grandparents or close relatives. But now everyone has been left out in the cold, as we've not committed to be near our families and are willing to be transient and move for jobs, only to find it's nearly impossible to make that work.

What does integration look like? That's the key question. And one we will come back to in a little bit. But first let's talk about cartels.

———

Cartels are brutal. They systematically destroy things—people, places, and relationships—so they can profit. They conspire and strategize. They affect everyone in their wake and cause untold damage for generations to come.

And there is one in particular that has had a generational impact on everything we know about daily life.

Specifically the Phoebus Cartel of 1924.[5]

Two days before Christmas, some of the most powerful businessmen on the planet met in Geneva and held a meeting, the results of which we are living with today. It was a group of all the top light bulb manufacturers from around the world— Germany's Osram company, Netherland's Philips, and the US's General Electric. Imagine a boardroom with all the top executives from each global and regional company and you've envisioned the Phoebus Cartel.

Their goal was simple: stabilize the enormously volatile electric market for more profit and revenue. But their way to achieve that was ingenious and innovative: make the light bulb worse and roll back decades of progress and innovation.

In other words, planned obsolescence.

The Phoebus Cartel was seen as one of the first large-scale efforts toward this. They strategically planned and created things that would intentionally and purposely go obsolete or stop working at a given point in time.

Planned obsolescence is building something to purposely fail, so the consumer will need to buy another one. And another one. And another one.

In 1924, while the household light bulb burning time was generally around twenty-five hundred hours, the cartel put rules and systems in place to make sure the bulbs would last almost exactly one thousand hours. And the cartel took this goal so seriously that the innovation and budgets and time committed to it almost matched the effort of earlier researchers who were trying to *extend* the life of the bulb.

In fact, all around the world, any factory bound by the cartel agreement had to regularly send light bulbs they produced for testing. If any light bulb was tested and found to exceed the one-thousand-hour lifespan, the factory was charged a fine.

Some of the wealthiest and most powerful corporations in the world had entire rooms and sections of their warehouses dedicated to testing the perfect failure point for their devices. Most notably, at the same time in 1924, there was another wealthy businessman conjuring up a way to get more money in a similar manner. While the Phoebus Cartel concentrated on making the light bulb stop functioning on a particular date,

Alfred Sloan Jr., the head of General Motors at the time, had the idea of making things go *out of style* quicker.

Sloan's idea was brilliant. He realized that instead of selling a car that was meant to last as long as possible, they could sell more cars if they sold the same car the next year but with the tiniest changes to appeal to people's desires for the newest model available. Before Sloan, most automobiles (including those made by the giant company Ford) were black. Sloan, by taking note from the bicycle industry, decided to introduce the magic idea of choice by coming out with new colors every year. And since then, almost one hundred years later, we are still enamored with next year's car even though it does exactly the same thing as the one we currently have.

And this matters because there is no better phrase to describe our culture's view of family than exactly how the Phoebus Cartel and Sloan viewed their industries: planned obsolescence.

In the West, *we plan for families to implode.* We literally have mechanisms in place to make sure they fall apart. Our entire system is built on the view that family *should* self-destruct—if you can supersede your family and no longer "need" them, that's a success story in America!

Quick question: Can you even name *one* great-grandparent? I've only met a few who can, but even they couldn't name a great-great-grandparent. I personally can only name one and have only met one of my grandparents.

Yet if you ask most Jewish people who their great-great-great-great-great-great-great-great (you get the idea) grandfather is, no matter where you are in the world or what country they are living in, they'd say Abraham. They know where they came from.

In fact, God seems to care about this too. So much so he actually chooses as one of his primary names and identities when speaking to his people a name that has to do with family lines. He says, "I am . . . the God of Abraham, Isaac and Jacob."[6]

Notice that when God himself wants to communicate his very identity, he doesn't choose a trait—like "God the powerful" (even though he is)—he specifically ties his name to a generational line.

If modern Christians were to write the Bible, it'd probably say, "I'm the God of I don't know, I don't recall, and I don't care." That kind of apathy toward our lineage is built into the system. It's why we do ridiculously weird things like calling the family a "nest," or when our kids leave calling ourselves "empty nesters." And we actually celebrate that term. It's seen as a virtue.

What a strange metaphor for family. Baby birds literally get pushed over the edge of the nest and fly or die, never to be seen again.

We want families to be built to last. But everything we do points to them being built to fail. Built to fracture. Built to implode. Built to self-destruct.

"Failure to launch" is a common phrase in the American lexicon (and the title of one of our favorite movies). (And let's be clear, the extended adolescence and lack of initiative among our children to enter the world as adults is a different problem, and not what we are advocating here.)

But the weirdest part of all this disintegration is that we actually think it's a virtue.

We think we are doing right by our kids if we send them off into adulthood to *start a new family*. Are they starting their own division within the team? Of course. But ancients never would have considered each generation as starting a new family, only adding onto the generational chain with a new link.

Of course it's not as black and white between modern and ancient. We still do family reunions and share family stories—in fact, I wonder if the surging popularity of DNA test kits shows that something in our hearts longs for connection to the past. But I don't think we have many mechanisms or tools to get us there. And it's certainly not the default. From my vantage point, the default is mostly delete everything before us and start anew.

For me, this gets to the root of why I was never excited to be a dad or build a family. I love to build, I'm a high visionary whenever I take those random personality tests, and I love to think of ways to implement my visions. So why would I want to spend so much time and energy pouring into something and building something that will just vanish into thin air in twenty years? Like, who wants to build something that has a self-destruct bomb written into its very code?

I'm convinced this is why it's so much easier and alluring to put most of our energy toward work and businesses and projects: we are inherently created to build things that last. We are built for legacy making; we are usually just putting it in the wrong places. And the very conduits God has graced us with to do that building—children—have somehow in our culture become the exact opposite: the curse standing in the way of truly building something. Huh?

Imagine for a second if corporations and businesses acted like the Western family. If every time a leader of the company was reaching old age, instead of passing the baton of the company and assets to a new generation and vision, he instead pressed the self-destruct mode. He got in front of the whole company and all its staff and said, "Okay, guys, we've spent fifty years building this company. We've spilled our blood, sweat, and tears, and experienced the ups and the downs. But now that I'm about to die and move on from this company, I thought it'd be a great time to sell all the assets, completely dissolve the company, throw away or give back all our patents and copyrights, and John and Katie (my son and daughter who work in the company) can now finally spread their wings and start a new company. It's their time to build something with their own two hands."

If I was in that room, I'd think, *What an absolute waste.* Like, seriously, how dumb would it be for a business to completely burn itself to the ground and restart every time a founder reached the end of his tenure?

I think we'd all feel the same. No, that's not how it works. You pass on what you've built, to be stewarded and taken further by a new generation. That generation has new ideas, new vision, new ways of doing things (they are not just servants marching to the beat of the last generation's drumming), but under the umbrella of a company name and a honed bull's-eye. Think how differently Tim Cook has been from Steve Jobs in this regard, but they are both still Apple.

It is just absurd to spend decades building something and then purposely self-destruct it. Yet in families we do this all the time. It's even considered a virtue! One practical way this plays out, but I think is a really good metaphor for all of life, is with inheritances. In our culture it's almost seen as an evil to give your kids an inheritance—it's enabling, setting them up for failure, and strips them of an ability to mark their own way. And if this doesn't reveal our culture's absolute value of independence being the highest form of virtue, I don't know what does.

The *Atlantic* headlined a recent article with "How Much Inheritance Is Too Much?" insinuating the bare minimum is the best—anything above that is "harmful," the article suggests.[7]

Or take Bill Gates who, in a TED talk, described passing his wealth to his children. He is famously on record saying his kids will each receive only $10 million in inheritance, something around .01 percent of his wealth, and his reasoning is, "We want to strike a balance where they have the freedom to do anything but not a lot of money showered on them so they could go out and do nothing."[8]

And so even there you see it: this strange belief that more resources equals *doing nothing.*

But the paradox that confuses me is that if rich people think their kids will do nothing with their inherited wealth, why do they believe the best logical solution is to give it to someone else's children? Because no matter how or who you give the money to, they're someone's children.

I believe the team mindset is the opposite: more resources equals more mission. But I'm not always pro inheritance. I do think wealth can be damaging for anyone living in a Western consumption-based society. If your kids are consumers, which most of us raise our kids to be, because our culture raises us to be, then it's a bad idea. We consume and eat and fill ourselves with every technological, sexual, cultural, societal, and emotional pleasure possible. That is the goal of life. And if that's our way of life, then yes, it's a horrible idea to give someone an asset, simply for them to consume and destroy it.

But I think the inheritance debate doesn't reveal that inheritances are bad, rather it reveals how steeped we are in consumer culture. That's why a trust fund kid is looked down upon in our culture—and for good reason, because we have created a consumer culture where assets passed down only means more to eat, destroy, burn, and waste.

In business, passing assets is seen in the opposite way. This is how you build really strong companies. Some of the strongest companies in the world have collected and built and expanded resources every generation. So why is it seen as a bad idea in families?

Here's why: businesses still center themselves around mission, whereas modern families are built around consumption. When mission is the focus, then building to pass something on is the goal. And a great idea. And so I think that is a much better picture of the biblical vision for families, including our spiritual lives. See, if you believe we are primarily meant to consume things, then resources become a burden—as they will only stuff that person with more and more. If you believe we are meant to produce things and steward things, then more resources should mean more mission and multiplication of what you're already doing.

We pass on our faith to our kids, not so they can consume it for their personal emotional feel-good, but so the territory of the kingdom (God's good and gracious reign and rule) can be expanded as we raise disciples who kick back the darkness and permeate every walk of life with the sacrificial love found in Jesus.

This is the genuine question to wrestle with right now: Do you really believe children are image bearers and conduits for blessing the world, or do you simply believe they are nice and fun yet inconsequential and actually stand in the way of the big things you want?

FAMILY SPOTLIGHT

The Owens Family

TELLING YOUR FAMILY'S STORY IS YOUR JOB

"You're pretty good at designing weekend experiences and events all the time since you're a youth pastor. You see people grow in short periods of time through crafted experiences when you take them away. Why don't you do something like that for your family?"

That was a question one of Paul Owens's church members asked him. And he realized he had never even thought of doing that.

Why?

There's something in the American narrative that allows men to give—or gift—their best at work but usually not for their home team, their family.

Like most turning points in life, that small moment struck Paul in a way that his imagination was sparked. He asked himself, *Yeah, why don't I do that for my family?* And it was through this reflection that he birthed an idea for a family storytelling retreat.

He realized he wanted his small son to know he was part of a much bigger faith legacy and family than just the nuclear generational story it's easy to believe in the West, so Paul decided to go out on a limb and craft and create a weekend where his entire extended family was invited to a retreat with one goal: to tell stories. Lots of them. And there was a lot of family—three living grandparents, the parents, his adult siblings, and all their kids. More than twenty people. He expected no one to say yes. He was intimidated and scared.

Everyone said yes. Everyone showed up.

Paul says he learned something surprising: "When we got done with this strangely intentional and intimate experience as a family, that you don't often find with your family, where we grew and got to know each other—what we found is *we really didn't know each other and this was supposed to be our family.*"

The grandparents got their own night, and he told them to come prepared. The night was theirs, and he wanted them to start from the beginning and tell their entire life stories— and then the rest of the family would ask questions.

He did the same thing with his parents, a dedicated night for their story. And guess what? It was not easy! There were tears. Difficult parts to talk about. Layers of vulnerability not everyone wanted to peel back.

But in the awkwardness, and in the discomfort, Paul began to point his gifts toward his family. Who better to craft a weekend storytelling retreat than a person whose entire vocation for years was to craft intimate and intensive growth experiences for others?

And that's what I love most about the Owens family story. Paul didn't learn a new skill. He didn't have to acquire new and different techniques. Of course he faced insecurity and difficulty (don't those always exist with family?), but he pointed his gifts toward his family.

What gifts do you have that others are getting but your family isn't?

FOUR

The Original Family Blueprint

Why does sticky webbing come out of his wrists? Why is he a billionaire who uses all his money to fight crime? Why is he in an alternate 1985 with an evil Biff?

These are all questions you probably would have if you jumped to the middle of the *Spiderman*, *Batman*, and *Back to the Future* movies.

But these aren't questions you'd have if you started from the beginning, what the comic books call "origin stories." (Even though I don't think the origin story helps me understand why Christian Bale sounds like he has a severe case of emphysema whenever he talks as Batman—but that's another question for another time.)

Origin stories are deeply important, and without them

it's very difficult to answer the why question. But a big why illuminates so many things. And we have an origin story in Genesis—one that gives us a compelling story to help make sense of, or at least be a launching pad for, myriad enormously large ideas: marriage, family, sexuality, evil, vocation, job, God.

The book of Genesis is important on another front as well. One of my seminary professors a long time ago said to remember the "law of firsts" in the Scripture. And what he meant was to pay attention to the first time a value or principle or idea shows up in Scripture, because that tends to show the original vision and set the tone for that principle for the rest of the narrative going forward. It's not a perfect law, but a helpful hermeneutical tip.

Which means the book of Genesis is more important than we think.

Even Jesus did this very same thing. The teachers of the law came to him with a very complex and purposefully trapping question about marriage and divorce from the Torah (the first five books of the Bible), and what did Jesus do? Everyone else would've argued on the face of their question and the finer points of the law. Jesus leapfrogged their point and went back even further: "At the beginning the Creator . . ."[1]

They said, "Here is the rule."

He said, "Let's look at the vision."

So let's do the same.

Because, as always, when we have cultural blinders on, we miss so much that is hidden in plain sight because we are reading the Scriptures as twenty-first-century, Western, post-enlightenment thinkers and readers. But the origin story is much more ancient and poetic and beautiful than the Western modern read we place on it. So let's do a quick retelling.

The story opens with heaven and earth being made. The creation was formless and void. Without shape or function or filling. And so God began to do what is inherent in his capacity as Creator: he began to create. Two ways specifically—to form and to fill.

He first gave creation shape and separation. Day from night. Land from sea. Then he filled it. With his beauty, goodness, creativity, and order.

And as the crowning act of this entire narrative and creation story, he made *ha'adam*, what we translate as man or humankind. And this *Adam* is said to be formed and taken from the *adama*. The *human*, taken from the *earth*.

Being formed of the earth points to two things: One, that we are made from dust. But a vapor. And two, our creative potential is what makes us unique—and truly to be made in God's image.

Just like the earth holds the potential to bear new things and new possibilities for that which is put into it, so we come from the *adama* and are given a divine vocation to harness that potential. We reflect God's image best when we continue that creative capacity. To bring order and goodness and beauty into the world where there currently isn't any.

But let's talk about that phrase for a second—image of

God. *B'tzelem Elohim*. The divine reflection. Or as some early Aramaic texts say, the icon of God. Divine diplomats granted authority, blessing, honor, and creative capacity under him. An incredible, certainly earth-shattering concept then and now. That every person, no matter what they've done or not done, has an innate stamp on them. No matter how hard we scratch, we can't get the image off of us. We reflect God.

One thing that is interesting about the creation narrative is how the *image of God* first shows up. It does not show up in some treatise about individual dignity (even though that's absolutely true). This image first shows up in the plural. In a group setting—or more appropriately, when a team is present.

> God created humankind in his own image,
> in the image of God he created them,
> male and female he created them.[2]

When God wanted to reveal himself in this poetic fashion, he did so in two symbiotic halves. He did it by making a team. He then put this team in the garden of Eden to work it and to keep it. This team was instantly given a job to do.

I think this is a place in Scripture a lot of us assume but don't press on enough. We picture earth as this incredibly ordered and tamed and fruitful, lush place. But that wasn't the earth after the creation narrative. That was a small space within it called Eden.

Basically, God didn't make the whole world look like Eden.

It's just a common conflation for us to read the more "zoomed in" account and think it refers to everything even in the "zoomed out" setting. He created Eden as a prototype, made divine diplomats as agents and ambassadors of his rule, placed them in this garden, and essentially pointed out to the rest of the earth and said, "Your job is to go make the rest of the world look like this."

The divine vocation and call is to build. To rule. To bring order and shalom to bear on everything we touch. And to do it justly, wisely, and lovingly. And that is the job we self-sabotage too, by the way.

But that job is massive. Go make the rest of the world look like Eden? We are still doing it to this day and will do so until we reach the new city at the end of the line. It's not a coincidence, by the way, that the Bible starts in a garden (Genesis 1) and ends in a city (Revelation 22). What's a city in its truest form? Just a bunch of "gardens" (places where people have made order and beauty out of nothing) all put together.

This is a massive, cosmic job. And so God says, "You're going to need a lot of help. Make sure to multiply yourself or else you won't be able to get the job done. Have a bunch of kids—or make a bunch of images yourself."

But let's look at it from God's perspective. He wants to fill the earth with his presence. It's in his nature—true love by nature *creates*. It is a cup that spills over. He's called *Creator* for a reason. So God creates and shapes and molds and spins into existence these beginnings. Of heaven and earth. And he intentionally only creates a pocket of order, called Eden.

Most of the earth at the time of the creation narrative was untamed. Unordered. Not fruitful or multiplying. And of course God could have made the entire earth to be so. But he didn't. Instead, he created a problem and commissioned his human diplomats to continue the work.

But something I love to do is pause for a second and reflect on how God chose to solve this problem. First, let's pretend we were in God's shoes—not always the best idea, but stick with me.

You have an entire section of the earth untamed and unordered. The problem is that it needs to be so. It is beginning to be brought into the symphony of created order and shalom, but it is not. Yet. How would we choose to solve that problem?

In the West there are many options. We'd probably create a business. Or start a nonprofit. Hire a bunch of employees. See if we could get a board of directors to give insight into the solution. Maybe create an app or tech solution to make it more efficient.

But did God do that? No. In fact, his answer was so peculiar, especially given no precedent. Out of the very mind of God the answer was to create two particularly unique image-bearing humans. Divine reflections of him, similar in image bearing, yet obviously not the same. And then he gave these image bearers the capacity to multiply themselves and have kids. And in that generational multiplying, the mission remains the same: order, shalom, beauty, fruition.

In essence, God's answer to the first problem in our story was *a family.*

And when I say family, by the way, I'm not sure I mean what you think I mean. Some hear that word *family* and think of a picture they have no way of attaining. That's not what I'm talking about. That's a cheap Western knockoff.

When I say family, I simply mean a "relational home," as my friend John Mark puts it. A network of committed covenantal relationships and a team that commits to one another and is interconnected through a web of long-standing relationships. It's layered and complex and older and spans generations. And having that web specifically work together and populate and bring forth his blessing into the world was one of God's original and ideal ways of being human. And this is good news because you can be a young single adult, you can be divorced, you can be old, you can be married, you can be whatever season you are in and you are a part of some multigenerational story—for good and bad. God wants to work through that and in that and in your last name. We easily run from our last names or stories, when God wants us sometimes to run into it.

What if we believed blessing could be unleashed into the world this way?

And let me be clear: this is not the only way to bring about change and blessing and goodness. That is obvious. But it is certainly something that seems central and primary, that is altogether lost in our culture, given our values.

Family is on the back burner. The last priority. Not the place we go for identity or mission or purpose (that's usually work). Our attitude is, who cares? Or better yet—why care?

Not to mention that a multigenerational mission sounds polar opposite of our highest religion in the West: speed. We want it, and we want it *now*.

But that's not how God works.

Family is the long game in a world of short and quick and fast. The West's long multi-century experiment since the Enlightenment and the Industrial Revolution and classical liberalism that our country was founded on is absolutely predicated on this concept.

Individuals' freedom and proliferation and uninhabited ability to say and do and be anything they want is the ultimate value. It is, without question, the most important thing to the Western project. Our culture falsely believes we can reach the utopia we are hoping for if only we can shake off any and all limits. Limits of lineage. Limits of team. Limits of corporate mission.

I will do what's right in my own eyes.
I did nothing wrong.
I am most important, not the other.

And we've been playing out that drama since the beginning.

The drama of God desiring to partner with us in divinely ordering and shaping his good world—yet the corrosiveness of selfishness allows us to reject him and reject each other.

It's almost as if we are team allergic. Why? Because teams get in the way of *me*. Or as we've been saying about the nuclear family, even if we don't think they get in our way, they most certainly should be about *me*. And making me happy.

But God himself is a team—have you ever realized that? That's the mind-blowing, incredible, uniquely Christian truth that God is three persons in one. And these three persons (Father, Son, Spirit) have eternally been in a relational cycle of love and harmony. And *out* of that cycle, icons were created in their image—aka us. And so, might it be that living in a team and not alone will actually allow us to be our best selves?

Think of any famous sports team. The relationship between the individual and the team is symbiotic. Steph Curry is who he is because of who he is *for the Warriors*. And the Warriors are who they are because of Steph Curry. The individual and team are not opposite sides of the spectrum but more like two sides of the same coin.

And you know what my favorite part of the ancient Genesis story is? God's original idea for blessing the world was a family team.

Yet sin happens. Destruction and decay and loss and the fracturing of all human relationships happens because of our disobedience and pride.

And yet.

God is unphased. Unmoved. In his profound creativity he still chooses a family team as the very way to put back the world as it was intended. The promise that started in the beginning and echoes all throughout Scripture is the promise to Abraham that through his *family* all the nations of the world will be blessed. Then through Israel (a big family), which apexes on Jesus (the ultimate Son) as he unleashes the church (the family of God).

The very people who broke it—a family team—are the very people who are going to put it back to rights. If that isn't grace, I don't know what is.

And personally, as Alyssa and I began this journey, this was the moment when things started to click. I was a young dad, one kid, in my early twenties, and it started to dawn on me, *Whoa. This family thing is full of purpose and blessing and identity and richness—if I let it be.*

And I looked at Alyssa and asked, "What's our mission? Why are we a family?"

And like most conversations with Alyssa, she knew that was a question that was going to mean a serious overhaul or a new future—and it was probably time to buckle up.

(Note: Anyone else out there move fast, I mean like really fast, when something moves them or clicks in their brain? Yeah, Alyssa knows that about me.)

And, after some back and forth and some study, I realized there are two buckets every family needs to put "mission" into for it to unlock their best.

First, as followers of Jesus, we like to say there are technically two missions for everyone. There's the *general* and then there's the *particular.* The *general* is the mission that every marriage and family on earth has been given. To be fruitful and multiply, and to *garden.* This is the general purpose of

THE ORIGINAL FAMILY BLUEPRINT

family, or what marriage and family are for. The *particular* mission is the very specific way God wants to apply the *general* mission in your family. The particular mission is the one that you and your spouse (and kids) have been brought together by God as a team to do and fulfill.

We've already covered lots of ground asking what was truly going on in Genesis, but let's go back there one more time and zoom in on one specific thought: "The LORD God took the man and put him in the Garden of Eden to work it and take care of it."[3]

God wanted divine reflectors, people with his image on them, acting as agents in his creation to worship him properly. And then he gave them a few commands, which only expand God's glory. Work the garden, cultivate and make beauty and goodness spring forth from your work, and multiply yourself as you do this so the territory can expand.

Notice how not even once were we told to just bow down and worship God via song for our entire lives. Yet our churches are nearly addicted to making this the high point of spiritual formation and worship. And let me be clear, this is important and true. But, at least in Genesis, it's not primary. Or another way to put it is, yes, we are called to sing to God but that singing happens through our vocation, not our mouths. Worship at the beginning of the Bible primarily was centered around the job God gave us. Our job was to make, cultivate, create, build, steward, and tame.

That is the original mission, the original mandate.

And then Jesus recapitulated this mandate when he stood there in his resurrected body speaking and commissioning his disciples. He was reinstating the original mandate, but with a new flavor, as the continuation of the same work—expanding and multiplying the loving and gracious reign and rule of God, being divine reflectors of his image and goodness, having our lives essentially saying, *This is what the King looks like. This is who we are ambassadors for.*

It's no coincidence that Jesus waited to reinstate the mandate until *full authority* was able to be reinstated as well ("All authority in heaven and on earth has been given to me. Therefore . . ."⁴). What a fun vision and mission, right?

Do you see the primary and general mission for your marriage and family as being cultivators, gardeners, and territory expanders of the earth as citizens of a heavenly kingdom that is slowly but surely permeating this earth? God brought your family together to be a team that was stronger together than separate, with one goal in mind: to do the job given in the beginning. To make stuff. And to show his grace, love, beauty, and blessing in it.

Many couples, however, don't think about the general mission given to them by God in the garden. They don't fully understand or absorb the fact that they are a team and a unit specifically brought together by the Creator of the universe to accomplish their job in a way different from every other couple out there.

Your reading this book absolutely is one of the conduits

THE ORIGINAL FAMILY BLUEPRINT

to repairing and continuing God's blessing in your last name, family, marriage, and generations. But why on earth would you believe it would be repaired and put back together in five minutes if it took hundreds of years to destruct and destroy?

God is a healing God. But I believe he takes the long way sometimes, because the long way is what lasts. Is what sticks. Is what speaks.

And so be encouraged that God absolutely wants to heal all the trauma and brokenness and pain and shards of metaphorical glass stuck in your soul when you think about the word *family*. But it won't be instant—it is more like planting an acorn that we are called to water and faithfully tend to, knowing our children's children might be the first ones to stand under its shade—and that it is worth the work.

FAMILY SPOTLIGHT

The Henry Family

STAY-AT-HOME DAD

Glen and Yvette had one kid and another on the way when Glen got hit with a realization. As he says, "I hated my job, and I also realized we were spending about 50 percent of my income from that job on childcare."

Like most moments of pressure, where new possibilities

can be forged if you let them, Yvette said, "You know what, Glen. I think you'd make the best stay-at-home dad." And like most good ideas, it was rejected immediately—with disdain!

And then she added, "And I think it'd be great for our kids to see what love looks like in those early years from their father."

When their family looked at their finances, the math was showing that they could save money *and* have their dad at home more if Yvette worked full time and Glen stayed home.

And my favorite part in talking to Glen was when he said he told Yvette, once he got past the ego side of the question, "Well, I guess. It shouldn't be that hard, right? What does a stay-at-home mom do all day, anyway?"

To which I, and he, and every parent now laughs. It's modern warfare—diaper style.

But that conversation was about six years ago, and the best part? You can see their entire journey through this online. Glen began documenting his "I have no idea what I'm doing but I want more fathers to be proactive and talk about this" journey on YouTube.

Six years later their family was handpicked by YouTube, and called out by the CEO herself, as one of the platform's premiere creators. And let me genuinely say, I think Glen is one of the most creative online originators I know. His videos about fatherhood and family and marriage are powerful and go well beyond the triteness of most other videos on those topics.

And it's from them Alyssa and I have learned deeply.

I asked Glen to describe the biggest misconception he had about fatherhood before he stayed at home. He said, "I used to think the best way to teach kids was to discipline and instill a small sense of fear so they'd be motivated not to do certain things again. But then I realized, the best way to teach them is to actually teach them. To get out the whiteboard. To draw diagrams. To play the scenario over again. To practice things like any healthy team."

And that sounds like a father coach, doesn't it?

In chatting with Glen and watching his videos (you need to ASAP, by the way—just YouTube "Beleaf in Fatherhood"), one idea that stands out to me is their incredible use of ritual and small traditions to build up their team.

For example, every morning the whole family stands in front of the same bathroom mirror. Glen says, "Repeat after me: *I am strong. I am not scared. Black is beautiful. Jesus loves me. God loves me. I am a leader. I can have a great day today.*"

Can you see how saying that every single day for weeks, then months, then years would have an impact deep in your soul? Reminding yourself before the busyness of the day, the anxiousness induced by the internet, and so on that you are loved. Known. Seen. And to do it together as a family is a powerful glue to keep the team bonded!

And then I asked Glen why he thinks their videos match the grittiness of life so well and capture such an authentic spirit when those of most other creators don't? And his answer still rings in my ears.

"Growth should look on the screen as hard as it feels."

One of my other favorite insights I learned from chatting with Glen and Yvette was their powerful steeping in the ancient principle of tactile remembrance of values. They let the kids feel them. See them. Touch them. Smell them.

And so I asked them for their absolute number one. What's one tradition or small ritual you think radically helps your family team connect or strengthen?

"Cutting the boys' hair," he said.

There is something about the touch and gentleness and care it takes to cut hair. There is a profound transformation that happens in the chair in your soul and mind—sitting down with your father, allowing him to shape and touch and gently groom you—that is an incredible picture of being a coach.

FIVE

Why Teams Are
the Way to Go

What would it look like to fight for integration?

My favorite definition of integration is *Merriam-Webster*'s: "to form, coordinate, or blend into a functioning or unified whole."

Can you say your family feels like that? Probably not.

Am I a mind reader? No. It's just, the system is rigged.

Because for the past two hundred years there has been a force fighting to do the opposite—disintegrate. Splinter, fracture, pull apart at an atomistic level.

Now *that* feels more like our families, right?

And there is a reason for that. Because to live a disintegrated life has one immense blessing and reason we do it: we can be more efficient—or so we think.

TAKE BACK YOUR FAMILY

Divide and conquer. Mindless work. Profit over everything. Dispensable. We are a culture of meaningless work and cubicles and underlings and corporate executives who have never seen a machine or touched the product they oversee, and whose only job is to make sure nothing falls apart while producing more of something, at less cost and with more margin.

Is there a better way? I think so. But swimming upstream always takes a little more work.

And once you leave the matrix, you start seeing it everywhere. This invisible force in our culture is actually pushing separation and fragmentation at all costs.

Major areas of our lives—like church, education, and sports—are separated and segmented by ages, almost set up in ways that parents and kids never need to interact, and certainly don't need to depend on each other. We break up our schedules and time and moments as a family in order for each person to get what they need (which is, generally speaking, a great and necessary goal, but we've gone overboard) without the family being needed or pivotal to any of those things.

Sounds a lot like Henry Ford's first moving assembly line and conveyor belt factory (which, by the way, I wrote about extensively in my last book, *To Hell with the Hustle*). Everyone in a specialty divided by parts and numbers and ages so we can produce cars that get out of the factory faster than before. Similarly, we hold a ninety-minute church service instead of a day of worship, prayer, and eating together, which is more like what the first-century Jesus followers did.

But did you know Ford himself voiced some dismay over his own creation? You heard that right. The man probably most responsible for ushering us into a more urban and consumeristic vision for the world also spent a significant amount of his time bemoaning the monster he created and wishing to return to the past.

But he didn't just stop at wishing. He literally built the past. Brick by brick. It's called Greenfield Village, and it still stands today. It opened just eight days before the huge stock market crash of 1929. And, according to historian Jessie Swigger, "Ford's vision for Greenfield Village was the culmination of a long-standing interest in the past, one driven by a complex view of the present."[1]

The man who played an enormous role in creating the monster of urbanization and disintegration spent a large chunk of his wealth trying to get back to an era his business was quickly erasing. He literally went around the nation buying old homes and iconic buildings, and then had them removed or taken down brick by brick, and board by board, shipped to Greenfield, and then reconstructed in a strange hodgepodge of nineteenth-century living.

He didn't model Greenfield after any particular town but instead started "organizing them around a village green with a courthouse, a town hall, a church, a store, an inn and a school. He placed homes along a road beyond the green. He brought industrial buildings, such as carding mills, sawmills and grist mills to the village and made them operate."[2]

If you go there today you'll see Greenfield structured around seven primary districts—with a fully functional farm, a glass-blowing shop, and a pottery-making studio as well.

Is it strange to anyone else that the man creating the flock to the city is also the man creating a fake antithesis? That the man creating more factory jobs than anyone probably in history was obsessed with recreating small trades and crafts replicas?

It's almost as if those closest to the sun are able to tell us how hot it is before anyone else. Maybe that's why Steve Jobs, the person who was responsible for creating iPads, didn't let his kids have one.

And I think I know what Ford was searching for all those years in Greenfield. A return to genuinely shared mission—something only teams have, but not clubs.

CLUBS VS TEAMS

As a kid I was obsessed with *Jeopardy*. My mom and I would watch it all the time right after dinner. I lived for the one-hour back-to-back of *Wheel of Fortune* and *Jeopardy* as a kid. So because of my obsession, when I got to sixth grade, I was dying to join the knowledge bowl club (think middle-school *Jeopardy* team) at my school.

I remember the first day of practice. I believe there were about six or seven of us. Because neighboring schools couldn't fill an entire team, there was no actual league or competition, and instead it was just a club where we would play against ourselves and have fun after school. Let me tell you, though, there is nothing, and I mean nothing, like the rush of a finger-sensitive answer trigger and buzzing in milliseconds before your opponent!

But you know what's strange? Even with the club being so amazing, and me loving it and being all about it, I can't even remember one kid's name from the group. I can't remember the teacher's name who led it. I can't really remember much about it at all.

After giving it some thought, I don't think that's strange after all. Clubs are shallower, softer, internally focused (instead of outward-mission focused) groups that only parody powerful and strong teams. And because of that they rarely get to the level of depth and memory and longevity that teams can.

And I think most families in the West are simply clubs.

Clubs are essentially a place to go to belong and hang out. You are not there to be connected or called up into a deeper story. You are in a club for you. For your fulfillment and personal gain. Everyone is. That's what a club is. (Think book club and other examples. You are there because it's a nice get-together and place to belong for a little while.)

And just like in a factory, in a club people are generally dispensable. Clubs are only held together through shared belonging and shared activity.

It's no coincidence our culture then hits the self-destruct

button right when the kid is about to go to college or enter the workforce. They no longer "belong" (the kid is gone and not in the home anymore), and they no longer share activity (he's at his job or school while the family is doing something else now).

Shared belonging and shared activity are helpful, but flimsy, glue aspects. Those traits can show up on a team, but they aren't all that's in a team.

Teams have much different DNA. Similar to farms, they are longer visions but collective missions. When Moses was recounting God's vision for Israel before they headed to the promised land, he wanted to give them a recipe for sustaining themselves long-term, so he said, "And you shall do what is right and good in the sight of the LORD, that it may go well with you, and that you may go in and take possession of the good land that the LORD swore to give to your fathers."[3]

When was the last time you heard that in a club? You don't hear those words in clubs. But you hear the sentiment in teams all the time. A pregame pep talk forecasts the seriousness of the mission and why you are collectively together. Teams *need* each other.

Think about all the things teams have that you usually won't find in a club.

Teams have . . .

Traditions
Secret handshakes

Uniforms

Insider language

Practice time

Game time

Obvious missions

A coach

Training

A clearly defined championship

And much more

See, clubs are primarily about the individual, but teams are primarily about the group. Clubs are about shared belonging and shared activity, but teams are about shared identity and shared mission.

No matter if someone goes off to college or leaves for a season, you can't shake an identity or a mission. Those stay with you as you go about your stages of life.

I can barely remember the name of anyone in a club I was part of, yet I can remember almost every kid's name on every sports team I've played on. Mission is glue. It's also not a coincidence people like the San Antonio Spurs, Navy SEALs, and even tech startups, when they are thriving and succeeding, almost always use language like "we feel like a family."

So is your family more like a club, where you think the only job is to give family members a decent place to hang out and belong, or do you realize there is something much bigger and larger and more fulfilling up for grabs, and nothing will be richer than when your family begins to work together toward a shared goal?

———

When thinking about the idea that the individual is called up into the family's story, and limits and sacrifice collectively can sometimes be very powerful, what comes to mind?

I'll tell you what comes to mind for me: a team.

Now, maybe this comes more naturally to me than it does for others since I essentially grew up with my primary identity and every waking moment dedicated to being a team—a baseball team, to be specific.

I started playing baseball when I was really young, and some of my earliest memories are baseball ones. I still remember my mom underhanding a ball to me when I was about four years old and me hitting it back to her and squarely hitting the mug by her feet, exploding that white chocolate mocha all over her. I still remember her saying, "Yeah, I think it's time we get you a tee now to hit off of, or I move back a lot farther."

Probably by age ten, baseball was central to everything we did. It was what our schedule revolved around. It was all I did in the summer. It was every day. Eat, sleep, breathe baseball. As some of you know, high school select sports are fun yet grueling and all-consuming. This all-in attitude was a given until all of a sudden, around May 2011, I was about to graduate college, and baseball reached an abrupt end. No more college meant no more college baseball team, and that was that.

I hung up the spikes that day, as they like to say.

And I remember thinking almost immediately, *What was all that for? What do I have to show for a specific dedication my entire life?*

I would say a lot, actually. Tools, ways and dynamics of working, but most of all what I never would've guessed is how much those tools have come in handy now that I'm building a family.

Why?

Because hidden in plain sight over and against the individualized model of family is the seed of the more ancient vision of family—and it's hidden primarily in two places in our culture: strong and successful sports teams and strong and successful businesses.

Here's a quick thought experiment. If an ancient father were to hop in the DeLorean and travel to our present day, and his mission was to find his present-day counterpart, the person he would be if he were around today, where do you think he would find him?

My guess is probably not at home. One quick look at modern fathers and he'd probably say, "Who's that guy?"

Joking aside, I think he'd most resonate with something like a Texas high school football coach.

Why? High school football coaches are beacons of the community. Well respected, honored, and seen as leaders to many, they spend countless hours planning and honing their skills so they can take their teams on a mission.

I think of my high school baseball coach, Coach Kuykendall. An absolute legend. I think during the four years I was in high school, we lost maybe six or seven games total and won more than one hundred (and played in two state championships). He was loved and respected and honored by many. It was an *honor* to play for Auburn High School baseball, and you felt it. What if we had that reaction about being in our families?

But it started with him. And I absolutely believe it was his father's heart that got us to that level of excellence.

I remember one specific moment when he pulled me aside after a bad game and said, "Jeff, this is baseball. It's a game. But how you respond to a bad game is all of life. I believe in you and want to see you make adjustments for this next game. Bad games happen, but your choice is how you will adjust and respond."

And it was true. And I remember that tiny ten-second lesson fifteen years later!

One of my favorite memories was a hot summer day late in the season. We were getting a little stale in the sense we were playing and acting like zombies. The grind of the same day, same practice, same thing every day for months had started to wear on our energy and minds and demeanor.

Right after we showed up to practice, Coach Kuykendall called a huddle and said, "Everyone follow me." So we sheepishly began to follow him off of the baseball field. Through the parking lot. Then onto the main street. And we stopped at a 7-Eleven.

"Slurpees on me," he said. "Everyone head in and grab one." And, as if that wasn't enough, he then said, "Okay, now everyone head back into the field, and take your shirts off. Let's work on getting rid of these farmer tans, and let's just have some fun today."

And for the next three hours, a group of high school boys had music cranked up as loud as it could go, shirts off (while probably yelling, "Suns out, guns out," because why not?), having a fun day of batting practice and hitting.

It was things like that that made him a father. He knew when to give you a heart-to-heart. He knew when to disrupt the order and ritual of things in a way that created memories and bonds and behavioral motivation.

Also, let me be clear, he was a fun coach. It wasn't just because he wanted us to have fun. I think he absolutely knew having fun, building a culture like that, created the team magic that actually led to better performance. And it showed!

That experience makes me think of Greg Popovich, the head coach of the legendary San Antonio Spurs, one of my favorite coaches of all time.

Carrot cake. By the hotel room door. That's what Tim Duncan, one of the most famous and successful NBA forwards in the sport's history, found time and time again over the years as he played for Popovich.

Carrot cake was one of Tim Duncan's favorite treats, and he had offhandedly mentioned it early in his career. And Greg Popovich paid attention.

So whenever Popovich was out to dinner on the road with the other coaches, usually at a Zagat-rated or Michelin-quality restaurant, he would ask for a slice of carrot cake. To go. And he'd drop it by Timmy's door on the way back to his room. For years.

And during Tim Duncan's retirement, what did Popovich say he'd miss most about Tim? "Taking him carrot cake occasionally."

It makes you wonder if one of the more powerful NBA dynasties of our last generation was formed not because of raw talent (even though that helped) but instead because of the million little moments of carrot cake and related things that make a team a family.

Or maybe the reason they were as successful as they were was because of who their coach was. Manu Ginobili, one of their best players during their run, said Popovich wasn't just a coach: "I think Pop was a father."[4]

———

But here's my thesis: I think families are all born to be teams and naturally have the gifting and wiring to do so. It's our culture and conditioning that works it out of us. Let me prove it to you.

Here's a challenge: find three of your peers and build the tallest possible structure with the following items:

twenty pieces of uncooked spaghetti
one meter of masking tape
one meter of string
one standard-size marshmallow

And there's one rule: the marshmallow has to be placed at the top of the structure.

How tall would you guess you'd be able to build it?

Thankfully, we have a pretty good idea—because a lot of people, teams specifically, have done this exercise.

This is a famous challenge invented by Peter Skillman in collaboration with Stanford University, the University of California, and the University of Tokyo. It had been done and repeated thousands of times across group variables.

Skillman gave the challenge to dozens and dozens of different four-person groups of business school students. After tons of trials, guess what the average structure measured?

Less than ten inches.

Not nearly what I expected when I first read this study, especially among some of culture's brightest and most elite. But the cool part is Skillman didn't just give this challenge to business school students.

Skillman wanted to look at various group identities and see who built the strongest and best tower, so he segmented and grouped lawyers, teams of CEOs, and even kindergartners.

And here's my favorite part. Over and over and over again, the kindergartners dominated.

They built structures averaging twenty-six inches (the lawyers averaged fifteen inches, and CEOs averaged twenty-two inches). This is *insane*. The people who were paid hundreds of thousands of dollars to literally solve problems day in and day out (in law and business) got defeated by five-year-olds. Not once, but over and over again. Consistently the kindergartners performed better than anyone else in the challenge.

Why? Skillman said, "The Kindergartners don't spend 15 minutes deciding who is going to be CEO of Spaghetti Corporation."[5]

Essentially, the kindergartners rolled up their sleeves and started working as a team. Everyone else was "distracted by status transactions, wasting time in search of control and power rather than acting as a single team."[6]

In fact, Skillman said the design challenge initially set out to measure and teach iteration and creativity, but the data was so powerful and consistent they uncovered much stronger lessons and connections about teamwork.

Daniel Coyle interviewed Skillman about the design challenge, and I love his brief insight and reflection showing this:

> The actions of the kindergartners appear disorganized on the surface. But when you view them as a single entity, their

behavior is efficient and effective. They are not competing for status. They stand shoulder to shoulder and work energetically together. They move quickly, spotting problems and offering help. They experiment, take risks, and notice outcomes, which guides them toward effective solutions.

The kindergartners succeed not because they are smarter but because they work together in a smarter way. They are tapping into a simple and powerful method in which a group of ordinary people can create a performance far beyond the sum of their parts.

There's no posturing among the five-year-olds. There's no subtle reads for who is a threat and who is competition. There is no status selecting. There is only getting hands dirty and collaboratively working together in energetic and dynamic ways.[7]

And here's my translation, and also the premise of this entire book you are now reading: *We are inherently built and wired for teams, and yet the West and our modern society inherently and systematically bake it out of us the older we get. The goal of the West is to never need each other.*

———

About three years ago, Alyssa and I, along with the Pryors, kickstarted the new venture you've heard about in this book: Family Teams, an online resource center to help equip families in their journey. We took these ideas online and began the Homeroom group mentioned earlier. Now we have thousands of families at different ages and stages, creating a sort of think tank where we can bring ideas to each other, sharpen each other, and opt out of this Western family experiment together. (PS: For the Family Teams tribe reading this, hi!)

Let's look at the story of Yitzach and the story of Brad. Both are twelve-year-old boys. One lived in the first century, outside of Jerusalem. The other lives in present-day America, outside of Atlanta.

Below are fictional interviews with both boys who answer a few questions about family and what it means to them, based on common historical and sociological realities.

YITZACH SON OF ASA

Yitzach lives in the village of Tekoa, south of Jerusalem. He has three older brothers, two older sisters, and one younger sister. His family owns twenty-three acres of olive trees and thirty-five acres of wheat, as well as eighty-four sheep and fourteen goats. They own a family home in the village, as well as a variety of sheds on their land. They employ three primary full-time staff, two of whom assist with the household and one who is an assistant foreman for projects. They also oversee anywhere between two and twenty seasonal employees, depending on harvest time and other peak seasons.

All of Yitzach's siblings live in his family home, which has different sections and apartments, including his older brother's wife and their two children, his great-aunt, and his grandfather, who is a widower and a village elder representing their family and serving their community.

YITZACH, PLEASE DESCRIBE YOUR FAMILY. We are descendants of Abraham, Isaac, and Jacob, from the tribe of Judah and the line of Jahab, who led our family in the war against the Greeks two hundred years ago. Before the Romans took over, our family owned two hundred acres of olive trees, but it's been hard as we have slowly begun to sell our land more and more to pay the heavy taxes put on us by the Romans. My father has asked me to learn a new trade for our family in case we lose the rest of our land.

WHO ARE YOUR HEROES? My biggest hero is Jahab. We still have his sword and shield hanging in our home, and my grandfather tells us stories about him and other ancestors of our clan every Sabbath.

WHAT DO YOU WANT TO DO WHEN YOU GET OLDER? I'm hoping to learn the skill of blacksmithing and to sell my wares and services to help my family keep our land—and eventually to buy more of it back from a Roman centurion.

WHAT IS YOUR FAMILY HOPING TO ACCOMPLISH THIS YEAR? We are hoping to save enough from the harvest and from all the lambs born this year to buy back one of our acres and to add on a room to the house for when my second-oldest brother is wed.

WHAT WOULD YOU LIKE TO ACCOMPLISH THIS YEAR? I'm learning ancient Hebrew from our rabbi and hope to honor my family by being able to read the Torah well at my bar mitzvah. My parents will also have paid for me to learn some valuable skills from Joseph the blacksmith, and I hope to bring in twice as much this year as last year by repairing equipment for families in our village.

WHAT IS YOUR BIGGEST HOPE? That the Messiah would return and bring justice for my family for all the suffering we endured under the Romans. I also hope that our home and land would be established forever and that our descendants will live in peace in the land.

WHAT IS YOUR BIGGEST FEAR? That we would be forced to pay even higher taxes and sell the rest of our land, and that our family would have to hire ourselves out to other families. If this happened our name might disappear from the families of Israel.

Brad Johnson

Brad lives in a middle-class Christian home in the suburbs of Atlanta. He is twelve years old and has an eight-year-old sister. His dad works as a regional sales rep for Proctor & Gamble and his mom works part-time teaching preschool. He goes to Roswell Middle School, and his grandparents on his dad's side live in Richmond, Virginia. His other grandma

WHY TEAMS ARE THE WAY TO GO

recently moved into an apartment near their home where his mom can help care for her.

PLEASE DESCRIBE YOUR FAMILY. Well, my parents are nice but a little strict, and my sister is totally annoying. My mom helps me with my homework, and my dad helps coach my Little League team in the spring.

WHO ARE YOUR HEROES? I guess a few of the baseball players on the Braves are pretty cool.

WHAT DO YOU WANT TO DO WHEN YOU GET OLDER? I'm not sure. I'll probably go to college and have to decide then, but I think I want to be a pro baseball player.

WHAT IS YOUR FAMILY HOPING TO ACCOMPLISH THIS YEAR? Uh, I think we want to go on another vacation to Florida this summer and maybe get a new car.

WHAT WOULD YOU LIKE TO ACCOMPLISH THIS YEAR? I hope to be a pitcher on my baseball team this spring, and to make more friends at school. I really hope I get the new iPhone for Christmas.

WHAT IS YOUR BIGGEST HOPE? That the Braves make it to the World Series and that this cute girl at school will notice me.

WHAT IS YOUR BIGGEST FEAR? That I won't have any friends at school and will be treated like a nerd by the popular kids.

Notice the difference? Me too.

97

SIX

Drafting Your Team

"I feel like I'm parenting all by myself!" Alyssa said with eyes filled with tears and hot anger.

Have you ever had a moment when someone accused you of something and you didn't argue or get defensive because you immediately felt a check in your spirit?

Alyssa was correct. And her emotions and frustration were exacerbated by the fact we were a few months into having our first child, and we realized how utterly fast it had all gone.

You know how when you get married people instantly start asking you when you're going to have kids? The question came at us so frequently we began to have this pretty cut-and-paste answer: "Oh, there are still a few things we are hoping to set up and do before we have kids, and our plan is to start trying in four or five years."

But ten months into our marriage, Alyssa didn't feel very

good and biologically missed a few markers, so our interest was sparked enough to get a test.

It said *positive.*

My heart said *fear.*

It certainly wasn't our plan to have a baby then, and we were young, considering the millennial marriage trends these days. I was twenty-three, just married, a baby on the way, and no ducks in a row—I didn't even know what the ducks should be!

Because of my personality, I started researching like crazy. That's just how I work. When presented with a challenge, information is security for me. I want to know all the research, all the data, all the tips. And my desire was to be a good dad.

But guess what? I really wasn't. Which is why Alyssa was still struggling months after Kinsley was born.

And that's normal!

Parenting is one of the highest risk jobs—you are caring for another human who is incapable of doing anything on their own—and you have no experience, no résumé, no specific training that can help you.

It's the epitome of on-the-job training. You can read all you want, learn all you want, and this is helpful! Trust me, it's kind of like giving yourself more arrows to shoot the bull's-eye. But you won't know what you are doing until you actually do it.

I think this is exactly how God made it to work.

Yet too many of us pull the escape hatch parachute before

the act of parenting has had its opportunity to deeply form us into who we are meant to be. What a dance and creativity of God—to form us more into his image as we are allowed to form the very images of ourselves given to us as a gift from him. It's a mutual dance of grace and love and purpose and service.

And I still remember that first year as a parent. The miserable failure and shame and disappointment. It felt like my default behaviors and habits were destructive or unhelpful to being a good parent, and everything I knew I needed to be better at or do more of didn't come naturally at all. And the first place it took its toll on us was with what I call the destructive nature of the "divide and conquer" philosophy.

See, I grew up with the mentality that you take care of yourself and you expect others to do the same. My mom was a superhero and one of the strongest people I know, but the simple inertia of poverty and single parenting puts you into survival mode more than you think. And what you tend not to do in survival mode is be mindful of others' needs, much less serve others. There is only enough time to make sure you eat and survive, and as a child grows more independent, an implicit understanding occurs between parent and child, as if saying, "If we both are diligent and take care of ourselves, then this will go well."

Over time I accrued unhelpful, self-crusted habits—of hiding emotionally, using anger when I really felt sad, having a lack of accountability—that didn't show themselves as problematic until I got married and had a kid.

And the way it started to play out was I would feel bitterness and anger if someone couldn't take care of themselves. It felt unfair. It felt like a breach of an unspoken contract I was living by—everyone *has* to take care of themselves. That's the rule. If you don't, you sink.

But what's helpful in survival mode in poverty is not always helpful in the rest of life, and this mindset begins to corrode a heart little by little. We are not meant to survive alone but to thrive—to flourish and serve and *depend* on one another in a beautiful dance of mutuality.

So when Alyssa and I welcomed our first child, and we felt the stress of all the normal triggers—work, marriage, financial pressures, an infant now making demands every second of every day—my facade began to crack.

And like most of us do in crisis or stress, I doubled down on my bad habits.

I thought, *Okay, the way to solve this is to take a much harder look at myself and take care of my responsibilities and what I need to do.*

And so I did that. I got up early to get my work done. I went to bed late. I stressed out about every little decision and thing I needed to do. *If I take care of this, and Alyssa does her job of taking care of the baby, we will get through this. Just grit your teeth and try harder.*

And so I started working harder and chasing all of what I thought was the way to handle the crisis, and I looked over at Alyssa. She was not gritting her teeth along with me. She was crying.

She was sinking.

She was not thriving.

And what did I do?

I put my problems on her: "You're not keeping up your end of the bargain. This isn't fair!"

And what she said then still rocks me to my core: "I never made that bargain with you. This is not how it's supposed to be. You're not on my team."

She was right. She had never agreed to that deal. In all honesty, I had never even spoken it! What better way to have a marriage thrive than an unspoken false paradigm laid on your spouse without them (or you, for that matter) even knowing it?

You're not on my team.

Those words will cut right into you. And they did. I wasn't. That wasn't how teams act. That was how individuals act.

It reminded me of the story of Navy SEAL Mike Koch and his partner, Nate Hardy.[1]

On February 4, 2008, Mike and his team began an assault on an enemy compound in Afghanistan. As he entered the compound, an enemy combatant was hiding in the wall he would walk by.

When Mike passed by, he was shot and killed.

Upon hearing the shots and realizing the loss of position, the team began to retreat. Nate, his close friend and teammate, escaped with the rest of the team. Unharmed and in safety.

But what did he do? He knew he couldn't leave a brother behind, so he went back in to retrieve Koch's body, and he, too, was killed. They are buried next to each other at Arlington Cemetery.

Why did he do that? He said Mike was his *brother.*

At its essence, that is what family is—an unspoken bond to work together as a team. And it proves itself in the hardest moments—when you are willing unflinchingly to put yourself in harm's way or sacrifice yourself for another.

Imagine if Nate had stood outside the gates, yelling into the enemy compound to his dead brother, "You can do it. I did my part, now do yours! Just try a little harder!"

Gross, right? Yet that's what I was doing with Alyssa, and what so many of us steeped in individualism do in our marriages without realizing it.

We demand our partner, or worse, our kids, pick themselves up by their bootstraps. But that's not how teams work. Every time you do that, you're just giving the toxic view of American individualism another point.

It's almost as if the toxic underlying belief in American families is that we want to *not* need each other. We actually train our kids to live with no dependency. How on earth is that honorable or commendable?

Imagine Tom Brady going into the huddle with his championship Patriots and saying, "Okay, guys, don't depend on me. I can't do anything for you. The quicker you learn to figure all this out on your own, the better. It's a rough world out there, so make sure you can bear it all yourself."

Or imagine a company putting a bunch of employees on

the same team but making sure they never depended on each other to get anything done. Individuals depend on themselves; teams depend on each other.

One is toxic to a family. The other is the lifeblood of it.

Our addiction to independence is something we absolutely have to assess in light of being a team. I know it was something I had to radically address early on in my marriage—as someone who has not just a fiercely independent personality but also has developed a coping strategy of independence after being raised in scarcity and poverty.

And worse even was the fact that whenever Alyssa would express this pain point, I'd respond with the classic line, "I'm providing."

Can I just say I hate the "my job is to provide" train of thought? I don't think there's been a more destructive lie to Christian fatherhood than the idea of "my job is to provide."

Because at least anecdotally, what I've noticed is that this phrase is essentially code for "I make sure the kids are fed and there is a roof over everyone's head and the bills are paid, so I don't need to do anything else."

There's an insidious part of that mentality I've seen play out with so many dads. "Providing" has become more often than not an excuse to not be present, coach your kids, be close to their hearts, mentor them, or play with them.

Provide in Western culture means to provide money. But what we really need to provide is presence, grace, gentleness, compassion, leadership, and more.

What most parents need to do is stop "providing" and start *providing*.

Providing only shelter, food, and basic necessities is not the only calling of a parent. That's the calling of a babysitter. Think about it: What's the difference between a coach and a babysitter?

One is concerned with simply preventing the worst possible outcome; their main job is to keep the kids alive.

The other is concerned with creating the best possible outcome: How can I help you flourish?

Generally speaking, a babysitter's job is to make sure a child is fed, has his basic needs met, and ultimately is safe. Safety is paramount for a babysitter.

Coaches do much more: they teach, coach, mentor, create vision, plan, and strategize.

TOPIC	COACH	BABYSITTER
Primary Concern	Create fully developed and flourishing players	Meet child's basic needs and ensure their safety
Primary Tools	Proactive strategies and drills	Whatever passes the time (movies, games, etc.)
What's a success?	Resilient, powerful kids who work as a team and win championships	The child has been fed and doesn't die.
Most important group dynamic?	The team works together and is cohesive and strong.	Team dynamic doesn't matter as long as individuals' needs are met.

What are they looking forward to the most?	Building a dynasty	The end of their shift
How do they see difficulty?	Tension and resistance build muscle and resilience.	If something is difficult or hard, we must be doing something wrong. Keep the peace and stability at all costs.
End game	The full development of the child.	Give momentary peace and happiness
Vision	Coaches care about who you will become ten years from now.	Babysitters care only about the present moment.
The kid's identity	Is given/fostered by the coach	Is not impeded on or developed whatsoever
When the kid asks a question	Teach	Solve

And here's one last prominent difference that I think all of us parents need to take to heart: coaches are experts about their players; babysitters are novices.

A babysitter might know what foods the kid likes, when he needs certain medications, and what his favorite show is, but coaches know how their players are wired. They study their players. And at some level they know their kids better than the kids know themselves.

I still remember this hitting home with a coach of mine in

college. He was a regional legend, had won championships, and it was an honor to be on that team and under his leadership.

Once during practice in the middle of a bullpen session, the coach made a comment that was brief and nonrevelatory on some level. He was watching my mechanics and helping with a few things, and he said, "Jeff, you don't trust your fastball or cultivate it that much, but you have a very powerful one."

Now, the general stereotype of a left-handed pitcher is that we pitch backward (we rely on curveballs and changeups). And I was the stereotype times ten. I remember I did this because when I was younger my fastball was really slow and mediocre, so I got in the habit of what I thought was serving me best. But as I progressed through college, did weight training and got stronger, I still kept my old style of pitching even when my velocity was climbing.

And in that bullpen session, he saw a vision of my true self—what I could offer and do—better than I could. Because he had studied me and knew my mechanics and capabilities even better than I did, he was able to offer me a better version of myself in the future.

And guess what? From that session on I pitched the best games of my life. I retained my bread-and-butter off-speed tools, while cultivating and trusting a much stronger fastball than I was used to pitching.

So maybe put down the book for a few minutes, reflect on your vision of parenting success, and see if it looks more like a coach or a babysitter (and the job of coach includes the babysitter's jobs, but it's so much more). Do you study your players? Are you actively taking your family somewhere? Do you have a plan and a vision for your family's future? Do you come alongside them?

Because this isn't just a theory or some nice ideas. And this came home to me in that exact moment of Alyssa's frustration at the beginning of the chapter. And why I was so upset at her disappointment.

I had been an *excellent* babysitter, hadn't I? Everyone was provided for. The bills were paid. The family was safe and stable.

Yet we were also drowning.

And it was in that moment when something awakened in me. I still remember that feeling of coming alive—that as a father I wasn't created to babysit, I was created to coach. And a light bulb went on. I was asking for applause because I was doing the bare minimum. But who cares about the bare minimum? God calls us to the maximum, and you'll only find true humanness and genuine flourishing there.

Maybe it was because of my sports background, or the way my brain thinks in an almost perpetual scribbling on a whiteboard, but that weekend I got out a piece of paper and wrote at the top "Family Scouting Report."

Now, for those who aren't familiar with that term, a scouting report is basically a mini-textbook on your players (or your opponent's players) so you can make informed decisions about the team. It'll have obvious things like weight, height, speed, and arm strength, but it includes even more detailed and nuanced info like "What does this player tend to do when scared or in a hard situation?" or "How does this player react when he strikes out?" or "What are his tendencies under pressure?"

As I thought more about scouting reports, I realized, shouldn't we know our own children this well? As a babysitter I had cared only about a few of my child's preferences—she likes this food, this toy, etc. But as a coach I would need to ask much deeper questions about my teammates—what makes their hearts light up, how are they wired, and what are their weaknesses we can help watch out for?

Alyssa and I began creating and using our family's scouting reports to name and solidify the different roles and wirings of each person on the team. That way, our team would be more well rounded and well balanced.

Today, our Family Scouting Report includes the names of our kids, and we answer these questions about each of them:

1. What's their role on the team?
2. How are they wired or gifted?
3. How or where do they need the most support?
4. What activities do we need to prioritize for them to flourish?
5. What is the best way to spend one-on-one time with them?
6. When do they come most alive?

We update our answers about once a quarter, and certainly at least once a year during our family summit.

I guess the looming question behind it all is: How can you be a family team if you don't even *know* your family team? I want to know my team, and I want to be a good coach.

When I finally saw myself as a father coach, everything changed in our house. No single idea turned us upside down (or should I say right side up) as much as that one.

Having played seventeen years of baseball and four years of basketball on school teams, summer teams, and camp teams, I don't even know the number of coaches I've had. Probably somewhere in the realm of fifty to seventy-five, with ten of them being so prominent in my life that I spent significant amounts of time with them. Maybe it was the grace of God or maybe it wasn't, but I have had a handful of incredible coaches, full-blown mentors and shepherds of my skill and development. And really only one terrible coach.

The terrible coach was one of my college coaches, and thankfully I was at an age and maturity when I could see through him (and actually felt bad for the guy). He was the classic movie character of the worst sports stereotype.

He swore every other word. Talked about girls and women in some of the most grotesque ways I've ever heard in conversation. And guess what his most used tool was? Shame. Yelling. "Oh, c'mon, that's terrible. Get out of there. You suck. What are you thinking?!"

But my good coaches? Life changing. We intuitively know

how a coach operates and how he can change a player's life when he's at his best. But here's the thing: only coaches are in this position of changing lives. And what's fascinating about those life-changing moments we receive from coaches is that they are often more subtle and smaller than we think.

Take Alex Pentland's famous experiments, for example.

If you are ever in a team or workplace environment and you notice everyone wearing lanyards with badges that are a little thicker and more electronic than the average plastic badge, there is a good chance you are in one of Alex Pentland's famous experiments.

Who's Pentland? He's considered by many to be the godfather of big data, and he pioneered an entirely new field called "social physics" at MIT's Human Dynamics Lab.

He essentially tries to blend experiments and questions dealing with human psychology and sociology with cutting-edge data and technology research. His most famous and most compelling work has to do with his sociometric device badge, which looks like a normal name tag except the badge is slightly thicker and has tiny computer parts inside that are constantly measuring more than a hundred variable points per minute.

The device tracks your location, and records interpersonal variables every sixteen milliseconds, that include, according to Pentland, "the tone of voice used; whether people face one another while talking; how much they gesture; and how much they talk, listen, and interrupt each other."[2]

What is being measured is basically how people say things

and act around each other, not what they are saying. The content (the technical words people are speaking) is not even being noted.

What's incredible about Pentland's device is it essentially quantifies and measures all the things we thought were immeasurable—when a team is clicking or there is buzz in an office, we always chalk that up to something ethereal and an "it factor," something you know when you see it or feel it but have no idea how to replicate, right?

Wrong.

This is where Pentland's work has been groundbreaking.

The research first started by looking at various teams—innovative tech teams, post-op wards in hospitals, bank teller teams, back warehouse operation teams, call center teams, and more. Everyone on all those teams got one of those badges. Immediately the data was stunning. Or as Pentland remarks in the *Harvard Business Review*, it had "remarkable consistency" and "in fact, we've found patterns of communication to be the most important predictor of a team's success."[3]

Let that radical idea marinate for a second. The single most important predictor their research found for successful teams was not how smart the team was, their personalities, the skill levels, or even the substance of discussion. Nope. Patterns of communication and how people interacted was actually a greater predictor—even more than all those other variables combined.

Now, what *exactly* do the badges measure and predict? Pentland calls them "honest signals"[4] because they are things that are nearly impossible for humans to fake. And the team with the most "honest signals" always outperforms the rest. What these honest signals always unequivocally do is create safety. They are the subconscious millisecond behaviors we are giving off that tell people lower in the hierarchy (boss to employee, parent to kid, and so on), "You are safe here." These are eye contact, energy, vocal pitch, consistency of emphasis. Things like interrupting, taking turns, and vocal tone all help (when done well) to signal "team, team, team."

Two of the more profound experiments Pentland conducted were in a call center and during a cocktail hour.

First, the call center.

He chose the call center because it's one of the most regimented social spaces in a work environment. He observed that call center managers "often try to minimize the amount of talking among employees because operations are so routine and standardized."[5] And so even coffee breaks were scheduled with precision, and they were always rotated—meaning everyone was given a separate coffee break by themselves throughout the day; this way the optimum number of people were always still answering calls.

Pentland then began studying and correlating his biggest metrics of the badge with what the call center measured and cared most about—AHT, Average (Call) Handling Time. This is the gold standard in call centers, where time is money. Better AHTs, which they define as "shorter," means more for the bottom line for the company.

What did Pentland find? Of the different teams and shifts throughout the day, the team that wildly outperformed the other teams had one big variance: they were easily the most social and did exactly what their managers did not want them to do—talk to each other.

With this information Pentland suggested an experimental change to the leadership—instead of preventing interaction, try harder to cultivate it and see what happens. He suggested starting by changing the break policy and making it so that everyone could have the same break at the same time.

The improvement in AHT speed was so dramatic that Bank of America did the same at all its call centers worldwide and generated a $15 million profit increase in annual productivity.

Not to mention there was an immediate rise in employee satisfaction. They wanted to work there more when they felt connected to their team.

Now take the cocktail hour. This one is my favorite.

Pentland and his team measured a business competition where a group of executives in small teams pitched different ideas to a group of investors (think *Shark Tank*) over the course of one weekend. But what Pentland teams brilliantly thought of was to host a "welcome party" cocktail hour the day before the competition started, where all the teams were hanging out, chatting, getting to know one another.

And this is truly the crazy part—without reading or even hearing any of the business pitches or ideas that came out that weekend, Pentland correctly forecasted the winners of the competition just by looking at the data from the badges during the cocktail hour.

The teams who were the most energetic, made the most eye contact, created safety through tone of voice, and used short bursts of communication (no one person talked forever) were the clear winners.

What kind of info would the badges record if they were put on your family?

Beyond honest signals, which are semi self-explanatory, Pentland meticulously laid out five distinct traits that top performing teams all have in common.

1. Everyone on the team talks and listens in roughly equal measure, keeping contributions short and sweet.
2. Members face one another, and their conversations and gestures are energetic.
3. Members connect directly with one another—not just with the team leader.
4. Members carry on back-channel or side conversations within the team.
5. Members periodically break, go exploring outside the team, and bring information back.[6]

Strong teams, according to Pentland, are enormously democratic, have frequent interactions, and do so in tons of short bursts (it's energetic), and—my favorite—which translates specifically to sibling relationships—its "members connect directly with one another, not just with the team leader."

In high-performing teams, basically everyone talks to everyone, but poor-performing teams are mainly top down, rarely side to side.

This is everything for families.

Why? Because sibling relationships matter more than you think.

And this is purely speculative, but it seems there is this American idea that your siblings are inconsequential. Almost accidental. And they don't really matter to your well-being or individual goals and pursuits.

But have you ever met any team, ever, who'd say their teammates are inconsequential?

In the typical Western home this plays out a few different ways. First, in fierce and toxic competition (there is good competition, but that's not what we are talking about here).

And this really shows itself every time a new kid comes into the picture. Either the team gets better, or everyone's piece of the pie gets smaller. It's one or the other.

I still remember in college when one year our team got a transfer student. He was from a Division I school, unbelievably talented, and got drafted the next year.

The only problem? He was left-handed. And a pitcher.

Why did that matter?

I was left-handed. And a pitcher. Which pretty much

meant my chances of being a starter were out the window after that. (For those who aren't versed in baseball, being a left-handed pitcher is seen as a tactical advantage—but if someone on the team has that same tactical advantage and is better than you—well, you get the point.)

Now, I could've been sour or bitter at first, knowing this transfer who was clearly much better than me was going to take up my playing time or my role, but I didn't. Why? Because I was elated he was on our team. I knew he'd help us win—and that year we won the regional championship. And I was still on the team, just fulfilling a different role.

Siblings are like that—teammates who bring a specific gifting and wiring that the family team needs. Which is why every time we have a kid, we immediately ask God, "What gap on our team are you trying to fill?"

What if pregnancies didn't scare us, or we didn't immediately think of the economic implications (even though this isn't easy, and is my default) but instead thanked God? What if we focused on the fact that this child is an obvious sign that he saw a gap on our team and decided to help us fill it? Maybe he knew we needed a tender, sensitive spirit to round out our family's rough edges. Or maybe he knew we needed a spontaneous, adventurous girl to help push our risk and comfortability? Or maybe he gave us a child with a brilliant mind to help us think critically through our family's mission over the years.

Another kid means another team member!

And that's how we should talk to kids about each other, with statements like, "Aren't we so glad God gave us little baby Lucy? I can't wait to learn more about her and why God decided to count us lucky enough to have her on our team." Or, "You two are siblings, not enemies. God gave you each other to be a constant friend, provider, and teammate for life that will outlast even the relationship you have with us parents!"

Something that can easily creep into most families is a sour spirit of competition. (Again, not talking about healthy competition here.) A spirit of resentment becomes subtly pervasive and each sibling begins to resent the other as someone who takes away more time, energy, and resources that are already so precious with Dad or Mom.

But it doesn't have to be that way. And it starts with the words and stories that come out of the parent's mouth. "Oh wow, our family needed you to better fulfill our mission God has called us to. We need each other." And that makes siblings teammates, not rivals, which is what a family was created to be in the first place.

Another thing: just because siblings are around each other 24-7 does not mean they are building intentional and thoughtful relationships. Ask any married couple. Just because you're in the same room doesn't mean you are connecting or being intentional. We know when that is. When there are shared hearts, vulnerabilities, and leaning into one another.

But why don't we cultivate that with siblings?

A family I know practices an amazing tradition of sibling

one-on-ones. They treat sibling relationships no different from date nights in their marriage—a time to carve out, be intentional, and build the relationship. But they are a family of seven, so that sounds complex, right? Their system is genius.

They have set aside a sixty-minute slot once a week when all family members do one-on-ones with someone and then rotate to another person the next week. So on Sunday morning right after church, they look at the chart in the kitchen, grab a soda or snack, and go find a comfy place in the house to play a board game or talk with their sibling. And the older ones who can drive take their younger sibling to a park or on a short outing. And just like that, in the span of 10 a.m. to 11 a.m., the whole family of seven has richly and deeply connected with each other, and the following week they rotate. Which means you have a one-on-one with the same person in the family about every six weeks (parents are part of the rotation too!).

But let's do the math there. First, this is only one hour every single week out of 168 possible. So it's not breaking the bank, per se, in regard to how difficult or time consuming it is.

One hour.

But that one hour adds up to fifty-two intentional dates between siblings every single year.

And over a decade? Five hundred hour-long one-on-ones where fun memories, trust, and camaraderie are being built. And it should be. Sibling relationships are the one relationship that statistically will be the longest relationship you have! Your spouse? Well, you knew your brother or sister probably twenty to thirty years before you met your spouse. Your parents? You will most likely have another thirty to forty years with your siblings after they pass away.

And as coaches of the team—you as parents—it is your job to facilitate these moments. Set the table. Put kindling on the fire. Do everything in your power to not just make the team a coach-to-kid group, but like the picture above, make it a multi-webbed and networked team among everyone. The strength of your team depends on it.

SEVEN

Same Enemy, Same Goal

Shake Shack is the best burger chain. By far.

If you disagree with me, or think it's something else like Five Guys, In-N-Out, or Whataburger, I will fight you (with words, of course). Because it's not even close. (Also, don't be that person who brings up some random, obscure burger joint. We are talking national chains here, people!)

But the reason is not just their quality and their ingredients (which do hold up). It's mainly because I love Danny Meyer, arguably one of the most successful and powerful, and more important, innovative restaurateurs in the world. His collective restaurants have won twenty-eight James Beard Awards, he has tons of Michelin stars among them, and he's started most of them in New York City, which is where restaurants usually go to die.

But it wasn't always this way. He opened his first restaurant,

Union Square Cafe, in 1985, now a pillar of the New York City food scene. And it was successful immediately, because of Danny Meyer.

He does things differently. He's peculiar. He is very particular about certain things. He thinks outside the box. In a nutshell, he has the magic touch.

And while there was pressure to expand into more locations or new restaurants once Union Square was successful, he delayed doing anything else for nine years. Because his father had filed for bankruptcy twice in his forties and fifties, Danny said, "I equated expansion with bankruptcy. He did too much—so I wanted to do one thing well."[1]

But finally he realized it was time. And so in 1994, he opened Gramercy Tavern. And his greatest fears became almost immediately realized. In the lexicon of the restaurant's storybook, the event that occurred was dubbed the "salmon crisis."

Both restaurants started to slip. To lag. To sink in quality. And it became clear that the reason was because Danny Meyer, the one with the magic touch, couldn't be both places at the same time. When he was at one restaurant, it was firing. Everyone knew what great looked like, and everyone knew what their coach hoped and wanted from them.

But the minute he left? They had no set operating principles, because he had never baked those into the system.

And then the salmon crisis put this problem past a boiling point.

At Gramercy Tavern, a customer ordered salmon. The

SAME ENEMY, SAME GOAL

salmon came out underdone and raw in the middle, which is not the end of the world, but she asked for another one or for it to be remade.

The problem, though, was that the server was disgruntled and didn't address the problem with cheer and spirit, but instead got bitter about a picky or uppity customer. So as the customer was leaving after the meal, the server packed the raw-in-the-middle salmon in a to-go container and handed it to the customer as a passive-aggressive way of saying, "This salmon was fine."

The customer wrote a letter to Meyer. And he realized this was a crisis for his restaurants, a symptom of the main problem. As the story goes, he began asking, "Who are we? Are we a passive-aggressive uppity restaurant in NYC or are we a place that people come to experience hospitality and warmth like never before?"[2]

And here's when I became a fan of Danny Meyer for life: he immediately closed both restaurants temporarily. He said, "This is not who we are, and this will not go one step further." (I don't know the inner workings of NYC restaurants, but I'd assume closing completely for even a few days would result in enormous losses in the hundreds of thousands of dollars.)

Every employee was expected at a weekend-long retreat. Where they argued. Asked tough questions. Confronted places of bitterness, resentment, and the wrong way of doing things.

But the main thing they did that weekend was come up with core values and a mission statement. Meyer realized the mission and core values that made them successful were in his brain, but had never been shared and institutionalized and thus had never been able to be scaled or passed down in a strong way that retained the culture he wanted.

All the employees left that weekend with five clear priorities:

1. Our interactions with each other come first.
2. Our interactions with customers come second.
3. Community comes third.
4. Suppliers come fourth.
5. Investors come fifth.

This, plus a few other core values and mission statements, was what Meyer and his team came away with that is now internally referred to as *enlightened hospitality*. And while this list might not look like much, it is a radical departure from conventional wisdom.

First, the number one priority goes against the axiom of "the customer is always right." At some level they realized this had gotten them into their problems in the first place. "The customer is always first" can create an impossible standard, and then the employees begin to subtly sabotage and commodify each other. Meyer argues that has to be the opposite, and it will naturally spill over to the customers. "There's no other way employees could outperform in front of customers if they don't feel good about themselves."[3]

Investors being placed as a last priority is a shock, but the truth remains that if you make the culture of the team paramount, everything else will be blessed and the effect will travel downstream.

After that weekend, when they developed both a mission statement and clear priority list of actions, Meyer turned his restaurants into an empire. And intentionality was the main focus. Check out some of these reviews from famous publications and notice how they *all* focus on how Meyer's restaurants make them *feel*, not just the quality of the food.

Bruce Feiler wrote, "Every gesture, every act, in a Danny Meyer restaurant makes the job intensely and unexpectedly personal. In many ways, being in an atmosphere of enlightened hospitality is like going to work inside your mother's fantasy of how the world should be."

Pete Wells, the head *New York Times* food critic, stated, "Another restaurant might try to impress diners by suggesting an esoteric sweet wine. . . . The servers at Union Square Cafe don't want you to be impressed. They want you to be happy."

Ruth Reichl noted of Eleven Madison Park, probably Meyer's most formal restaurant, that it is "personable, passionate, extremely sweet."[4]

It's probably not overstating it too much to say that a salmon crisis in the early '90s and a leader who dropped everything to ask the right questions led to one of the more successful restaurant empires in the world. It goes to show how powerful, and necessary, it is for every team and group to answer questions like:

- What is our mission?
- What is important to us?
- Why are we here?
- Why do we exist?
- What differentiates us from others?

If you don't know the answer to those questions, you might go bankrupt (emotionally, physically, spiritually, and so on)—but if you can answer them, you'll be able to make an impact and find the flourishing we are all looking for.

———

Alyssa and I had our own little salmon crisis about seven years ago.

We had been married about a year. We didn't have kids yet. And we felt strangely purposeless and without direction.

I don't know if you've ever suffered an existential crisis before, but let me tell you, it's not pretty. I basically woke up one morning with persistent why questions banging in my head and I couldn't shake them.

Why were we living where we were?
Why was I doing what I was doing?
Why was Alyssa doing what she was doing?
Why did I wake up this morning?
Why were we married?

Why did we not know any of these answers?

Why did I say yes to some things and no to other things?

Why am I here?

Okay, true, that last one is much more existential than the rest, and I wasn't asking it outright, but it was a byproduct of the others. For some reason I can't explain, that day I woke up feeling like I had been tubing down a river taking a nap for years, only to wake up and wonder where the heck I was, why I was moving in this direction, and what the point of it all was.

I had basically said yes to every good opportunity that came our way the year before we got married and during the first year of our marriage, and it was starting to bite us. (Anyone else suffer from imposter syndrome? I was convinced I didn't belong and needed to say yes to as many things as possible before people found me out and everything dried up.)

I was traveling like crazy (because I literally said yes to every request and invite), to the point where one time I flew home, landed at SeaTac airport, and instead of leaving I stayed there for a few hours to wait for my next flight for my next trip.

Not to mention I was helping co-lead and pastor a young adults weekly gathering of a few hundred college students. Burnout was lurking and right behind our shoulders. And worse, it felt like we didn't have much to show for all the work. I was just spinning plates and running in place.

That's when I called an all-hands-on-deck meeting with Alyssa that I still remember years later.

Note to other spouses out there: Beginning a conversation with "Why are we even here?" and "Why do we exist?" might not be the best start, depending on your spouse. When I asked Alyssa these questions, her eyes got cartoon big and she basically froze, completely ruining my belief that I'd just asked some killer questions to open up some spicy and fun conversation (lesson learned).

But once the initial shock wore off, I think what was surreal to us was that we had never genuinely leaned into those kinds of questions beyond surface level. We had never asked those questions in a substantial way, so we began to journey and journal through them before the Lord over many months.

Almost every family in the West, if you ask them the questions given above, would probably answer with, "I don't know."

But ask any sports team? The coach can almost immediately give you an answer: "To develop boys into men of integrity, and compete biblically" (this was one from a team I played on specifically) or "to win the league championship," and so on.

Or ask a successful business? They'd probably start answering before you even finish asking the question—relentlessly give customers the most compelling shopping experience possible (that's Nordstrom), or spread compelling ideas (TED), or one of my personal favorites, build the best product, cause no unnecessary harm, and use business to inspire and implement solutions to the environmental crisis (Patagonia).

Yet none of our families have an answer. We have no guiding principles. No North Star to point ourselves and our kids to. No framework to discern the will of God for specific assignments as his ambassadors.

And so we default to the collective American mission statement—consume more, obtain more, get more, and always be making personal fulfillment and happiness the chief aim of every endeavor.

Do you believe you, your spouse, and your kids (if you have them) are a team? A unit particularly drafted and brought together by God in a way that every team member's gifts and talents and personalities (and even weaknesses!) come together to give your team an identity to fulfill God's mission?

Let me tell you three quick stories, and let's see if you can spot any differences, specifically in regard to identifiying each team's enemy in the story.

———

Twelve-year-old Mary Goble and her family had been traveling from Europe to the United States, and over the course of months were finally in Iowa City to begin their final leg—but the hardest one. They were to set off on foot from Iowa City to settle in Utah Territory in 1856. The plan was to do so by hauling handcarts carrying all supplies, rations, and belongings, as oxen and wagons were too expensive for them. They were one among many families during this time making the same trek.

Tragically, due to conditions, Mary's two-year-old sister died and her family endured severe winds, a rainstorm, and loss of shelter—all before even leaving Iowa City. But they still continued. They were going to make it.

Her sister Edith was born on the trail, yet sadly only lived six weeks. They had to dig a grave by the roadside, which Mary at first refused to leave, fearing that wolves or Indians would desecrate it. Her father was able to convince her to continue.

On one occasion, her mother became ill and asked Mary if she would go to a spring nearby and get her some water. Mary got lost and couldn't find her way back. The company began to search for her and found her late that night, with her feet and legs frozen.

But it was noted that the Goble family and those traveling with them were all *in it together.*

"The Gobles shared the lack of food and the freezing weather along with others in the ill-fated companies, although her father was a good hunter. When they were stranded by snow and cold at Devil's Gate, an ox fell on the ice and was slaughtered and shared in the camp."[5]

That night Mary wrote in her journal, "My brother James ate a hearty supper and was as well as he ever was when he went to bed. In the morning he was dead." And despite her mother making some small recoveries as well, "she died on the 11th of December between the Little and Big mountains."

Mary wrote, "We arrived in Salt Lake City at nine o'clock at night on the 11th of December 1856. Three out of the four that were living were frozen. My mother was dead in the wagon. Bishop Hardy had us taken to a house in his ward and the brethren and the sisters brought us plenty of food. We had to be careful and not eat too much as it might kill us. We were so hungry."

Besides Mary having frostbitten toes that were immediately amputated (with a kitchen knife), they had finally made it.

Years later in Salt Lake City, Mary met Richard, a fellow traveler whose wife and newborn had died; they settled down and became ranchers. They had thirteen children, and Mary lived to the age of seventy.

Mary's story was not unique. There were hundreds of people on that specific journey, not to mention many others during the time when people explored the West. And while it certainly is a dramatic story, it's not unique in the difficulty known to those families. Before modernity, life was extremely difficult across regions, geographies, and cultures.

It's not hard to understand why Thomas Hobbes so famously called life "solitary, poor, nasty, brutish, and short" two centuries before.

Let's look at another story. A story about one of the more competitive and long-standing high school football rivalries in the country.

———

McDonough and Gilman high schools in Maryland have maintained a rivalry that goes back all the way to 1914.

Jeffrey Marx shadowed Gilman's team during the 2001 season and wrote *Seasons of Life* about Gilman High's coach, Joe Ehrmann.[6]

"As your coaches, what is our job?" Coach Ehrmann asked his players before every game.

"To love us!"

"And what is your job?"

"To love each other," they would say.

It's not very often you'll walk into a high school football practice and hear a group of sixty or so fifteen- to eighteen-year-old boys yelling this to each other. Ever.

Marx noted this beautiful distinction Ehrmann made between a goal and a purpose, and how the team had both.

The goal for that year? To win the division, specifically to beat McDonough.

The purpose of the team? To combat what Ehrmann called "false masculinity" and its three components of athletic ability, sexual conquest, and economic success.

And it's that goal and purpose that Ehrmann drove home day in and day out. During two-a-days in the summer. During the long, hard practices during the school year. And in all the moments in between.

How often do you see a coach, especially one ranked as the best in the entire state, say that the particular enemy and purpose of his football team is to attack the three lies of false masculinity? Not often, I'm guessing.

But it's because of those exact things Joe has become a

legend. Transforming hundreds and thousands of young men's lives for decades.

Oh, by the way, their team beat McDonough that year with a thirty-seven-yard field goal with one second on the clock.

They met their goal that year. More important, they found their purpose.

———

Story number three.

It was the first week of April 2020. The shelter-in-place order due to COVID had been in effect for a few weeks. All my travel was canceled, including an eight-city bus tour that should've been happening that very week.

Alyssa, as a homeschool mom, had multiple school outings planned to various public museums and bookstores that all got canceled for that month. And the book she was working on experienced delays and month-long shifts in the schedule.

And guess what? A poisonous, subtle spirit began to creep into our marriage almost immediately. You know, the spirit that asks questions you don't even want an answer to; you're just using questions as weapons or accusations.

"Why do you always leave the cupboards open when you make something for dinner?"

"Can you stop making us late to everything?"

"Why are you so selfish sometimes? I feel like you don't even hear me."

TAKE BACK YOUR FAMILY

And my personal favorite (read: the worst question, the one that comes out when I'm at my worst): "What are you even doing?"

And thankfully, Alyssa has a way of being able to jar me out of these moments sometimes—in humility and grace—by calling a pause. "Are you okay? What's really going on here?"

And that's when it hit me—we had, overnight essentially, lost, or at least shifted significantly, all the things in our life that were giving our family and marriage and vocation purpose and mission. Our mission is hospitality—but we couldn't have anyone over for dinner. Our mission is often to go places and teach workshops and meet you all—and all of a sudden we couldn't.

———

Notice any differences in the three stories recounted above?

Here's what I do want you to see:

The first two teams (the Goble family and the Gilman High School football team) had one thing in common: an obvious shared enemy. They were a team *because they were collectively fighting something.*

The Goble family, like most families before modern times, had the obvious enemy of the brutality of the world. The enemy was death, disease, famine, decay. Families literally couldn't survive unless they stuck together and worked together.

The Gilman football team? Their most obvious enemy was

McDonough, their rival. But Coach Joe made it clear the true enemy they were fighting was false masculinity.

But our family last April? No enemy. Fighting nothing. *Except each other.*

And it reminded me of the counterintuitive reality that sometimes difficult things—that you'd never wish on yourselves—have the power to bring together a family like nothing else.

For example, I think of an exact opposite story about our family the year before.

We had a business relationship that went sour. And when I say sour, I mean *sour.* Someone really close to us, someone intimately involved in our lives and businesses, all of a sudden took a sharp left turn—away from integrity, away from wise decisions, away from any ground rules you'd expect. And separating cost us dearly—our life savings at the time, not to mention losing a close friend and an important relationship.

In fact, I don't know if I've ever felt something so viscerally in my stomach. I couldn't eat; I couldn't even come out of the bedroom for a few weeks. It felt like a cloud hung over us and it was on my mind 24-7—with consequences that were relational, financial, and spiritual. I would wake up and cry sometimes from this soul-crushing feeling.

But you know what?

I can't pinpoint any other time in our family or marriage when we felt closer. I can't pinpoint a time when I've leaned on Alyssa more. For strength. Wisdom. Encouragement.

We'd pray together. Confess to each other. Look in each other's eyes and confirm absolutely that the Lord would walk us through this. Not to mention the tender grace of God I experienced when our children saw me crying and then walked over, hugged me, or began praying for me. (And let's not act like we have Mother Teresa children—the prayers were something like, "God, I pray for Daddy to not be sad. And I pray we can have cookies today.") But their prayers and encouragement made us feel like we were a team.

Do I wish that kind of betrayal to happen again? No, not for a second. But there is a strange truth to the fact that the most difficult times on a team can also be the most forming, bonding, and strengthening. Why? Because during difficult moments it's very easy to identify the enemy! And a common enemy unifies and strengthens a team.

It's why the paradox of war is so interesting, as shown and studied by Sebastian Junger in his shattering book *Tribe*. War is brutal, grotesque, and devastating. He does not romanticize it at all. But war fundamentally does something to collective groups that doesn't happen many other places. Crisis and conflict cause us to relate to each other in a way that our individualized society doesn't often motivate us to do today.

For example, after the Blitz on London during World War II, specialists projected that up to four million civilians would have psychological duress and breakdowns—and they began to plan accordingly for after the war. Yet psychiatric admissions fell drastically, and they even found that "strangers formed self-organizing communities in bomb shelters." Or take the fact that Ireland suicide rates dropped by 50 percent during periods of riot, or mass shootings in the US plummeted after 9/11.[7]

One of the more jarring examples and powerful moments from Junger's book was an interview with Nidzara Ahmetasevic, a teenager at the time of the Siege of Sarajevo during the Bosnian War in the 1990s. It was a brutal conflict—with more than 20 percent of the population killed or wounded. Nidzara was wounded when she was seventeen—when a Serb tank round directly hit her parents' apartment. And because of the war conditions, there was no anesthesia, so her leg was operated on for reconstructive surgery with her awake. But what she said to Junger was shocking to him, to me when I was reading, and even to herself: "The siege was so hard. It was terrible. But you know what? We all kind of miss it."

Junger wrote, "She then lowered her voice to a whisper because she was so embarrassed by the thought. And so I asked her about it."

She answered, "We were better people during the siege. We helped each other. We lived more closely. We would have died for each other. And now, you know it's peaceful. We're a wealthy society. And everyone just lives for themselves. And everyone's depressed."

In the same way humans can't live without oxygen, teams can't live without missions and shared enemies. And let me be clear: sometimes the enemy is tiny! One of the most random and fondest and smallest ones I can think of was right when we started to find our stride post-COVID as a family. And you know what the enemy was? The soil. We took up gardening as a family, and something about the shared collective focus and energy outside of ourselves toward the shared goal of gardening provided a conduit for so much more than growing vegetables.

One thing I think we need to be very careful of as parent coaches is not to let this creep happen among our kids. Because we are built to be on a team. It's in our DNA. And so if our family isn't the team, then our kids will just find another.

Psychologists Gordon Neufeld and Gabor Maté call this "peer attachment" and label it as a Western crisis in their groundbreaking book *Hold On to Your Kids*.[8] And it's pretty obvious to spot. In general, kids in the West are around their peers more than almost any other society previously, and around their parents less than any other society previously. What did we think was going to happen? Basically, their thesis is that a child's heart only has room for one supreme attachment (and it only takes one supreme attachment in an adult of health and love and warmth to combat and mitigate so many traumatic things!), but more often than not, our children are being peer attached and led.

And this has devastating consequences. In one of the more striking parts of the book, Maté and Neufeld make a compelling argument about why we should take this very seriously.

If your spouse were to go from warm, loving, and connected

(healthily attached) to bitter, mean, resentful, secretive, and standoffish, what would you automatically assume 99 percent of the time?

One word: *affair.*

Right?

In fact, psychotherapists have noted a handful of specific behaviors in adulterers that tend to show up every time:

1. They begin to become secretive.
2. There is an intense infatuation or chemistry with a new person.
3. They begin to complain about their spouse to this new person.
4. They have little energy or time for their spouse.[9]

And so Maté and Neufeld's obvious yet shattering question is, why on earth do we let every single one of our teenagers do this exact same thing and just brush it off by saying, "Oh, they are just being a normal teenager"?

No, all of a sudden becoming secretive or having a disdain for their own parents is not in any sense of the world "normal teenage behavior," and in fact, they argue, they are having an affair—what they call "an attachment affair."[10]

They have switched teams, and the parents have become the shared enemy among the group they are truly now attached to: their peers.

I think what shocked me the most from Maté and

Neufeld's work was what can help prevent it—and how small those behaviors could be. The key wasn't huge behaviors, but small, daily, faithful depositing.

For example, one of the tiniest and yet most helpful ways of preventing this in children, they found, was what they call "gathering." A strong, simple two-second eye-to-eye moment before you separate with that kid (such as before they go to school) and that exact moment you see them again (such as when they get home). A "we are a team, I love you, and we are in this together" can be communicated in a simple, fierce eye-contact moment that lasts for only a split second, they argue. And done daily, it powerfully becomes a glue to hold a kid together.[11]

And want to know what's funny?

Coach Ehrmann does the same thing, on purpose, when he starts every single practice with his boys—and has for decades. He even noted, "I want to make sure I'm the first person they see when they step on the field and that boy am I glad they are here."[12]

Makes me wonder if Coach read the same book. But it's those small acts of team creation that do more than most of us parents think.

EIGHT

Family *on* Mission

You know, I'm not much of an idealistic person. There's something about grand vision and lofty goals that tend to make me think, *But how do we make an impact or do something today?*

And it was for that reason that I resisted creating a family mission statement for so long. I had these conjured-up images of a family mission statement being nothing more than a cute Etsy printout meant to give the home a cool and artisanal design or look. It wasn't until years into our marriage and family that I started to realize that it was *vital.*

What company has any success if they don't know where they are going?

Who has ever done anything worthwhile if they don't know why they exist?

What team has ever won anything that hasn't declared over and over again specific goals and direction?

A family mission isn't something to hang up on our wall because it looks cool; it should be the very filter to drive every single small or large decision as you all navigate what God has for your team in this season, year, and life. A mission statement can be magical. It unlocks everyone's energy and focus and potential in so many ways. Because what it does is let your body and attitude fall into place once expectations and assignments have been set.

And you know what? It's saved us. From bad decisions. From bad direction. It's given hope and words in seasons when we needed them most, and specifically it's given language for the kids to rally around to know what our team is about.

Here is our mission statement: "We exist primarily to fulfill Jesus' words by living out 'your kingdom come, your will be done, on Maui, as it is in heaven' in our family, neighborhood, relationships, vocation, and all that we do."

We then have eight pillars, we call them, that guide us to specifically fulfilling that mission. Those eight high values for our team are:

1. We apprenticeship to Jesus.
2. Family is a team sport.
3. We center the table in everything.
4. Nothing is ours. We are generous.
5. Create more than we consume.
6. Live rhythmically.

7. Live multigenerationally.
8. Practice holistic health.

And guess what?

It took us about three years from when we first heard of this concept and got excited about it to actually writing down a mission statement and making it central to our culture as a family and marriage. There's no timeline or deadline, and in fact I recommend taking some serious time to sit and let things like this marinate before writing something down and calling it good. This isn't about making a cute decoration; this is about your family not perishing for lack of vision. And that takes time.

Now comes the fun part! The list of questions below is not exhaustive, and you also can't go through them and then say, "Okay, sweet, we have a mission statement, and we are going to have a perfect marriage starting tomorrow." That's not how it works. These questions and small exercises are better thought of as kindling to a fire. Mission statement conversations are not meant to be open and closed, but should instead be open-ended conversations that are malleable over the years.

For example, one big season during which the particular vision would probably change is when a couple has been married twenty or thirty years, and all their kids are out of the house. Their mission would need to be altered and adapted by seeking God's face and heart while asking, "What does he have for us now? What season are we entering into?" We revisit and adapt or tweak our mission statement at the end of every year.

Also note, a mission statement comes in many forms. It can be a paragraph that's beautiful and perfectly worded. It can be seven words that represent the seven pillars you feel your marriage is called to. It can be bullet points. It can be poetic or it can be straight to the point. Or it can be a mixture of both. Feel free to word it however you like. The key is putting to paper the things you feel called to and are passionate about to guide the ship and create a legacy for your family. This is a tool for your family, no one else.

Ask each other these few questions to get the ball rolling:

- What is different about our marriage?
- What other marriages do you really respect? Why?
- What is important to our marriage?
- What kind of marriage do we want to have?
- If others talk about our marriage, what do we want to be known for?

But let me say one word of caution, since we have worked with thousands of families trying to navigate the mission and purpose season of their families: it's important to distinguish between assignments and mission.

Mission is higher level. It's all the stuff we've been talking about. Overarching purpose and words and ways in which you can easily tell your family is wired. Maybe hospitality is your mission or being a generational bridge of healing is your mission.

But assignment? That's giving your values a vehicle. That's granular. And it should change often and have beginning and end dates.

Hospitality might be your family's mission, but giving your values a vehicle would be saying, "We are going to have an open invite to our family table every Thursday night to our kids' friends and our neighbors for all of 2021." That's an assignment.

Alyssa and I find ourselves using the language we are indebted to when we talk about seasons. We give every single season a name and an assignment, usually quarterly. And we've found three months is the perfect amount of time—it's just short enough where if it goes bad we won't burn out or be spending too much time on it, and just long enough where we can commit to it and it affects our daily lives in an overarching way.

So we name the seasons via our assignment: This is a harvest season. This is a "put our head down and work hard" season. This is a "rest up and recharge" season. This season is to learn a new skill and grow as a family.

You get the idea.

But let's be honest—there are still a few pitfalls when it comes to family and mission.

There are three general buckets families gravitate toward concerning family and mission. Meaning, how they see family and mission coexisting generally defaults to one of these three ways. And two are, I would argue, egregious missteps that we have to watch out for, because they can easily overtake a team and lead us down the wrong path.

I call the first one the Billy Graham Way. Now, first let me say I'm so thankful for Graham's spiritual legacy. What a giant of the faith, and how many folks do we know who would've remained so pure and faithful and have virtually no scandal in the limelight and next to power for that long? I don't know many. I also feel like I need to say that I'm not trying to pick on the Graham family by any means, but I know that their story represents an entire generation of leadership that has made the same misstep, and whenever that is true historically, we want to thank God for the power and impact that did come through, but also ask humbly, "What can we learn? How can we make sure we don't repeat the same mistakes, that even they themselves noted?" Can we ask where the ancient paths are and where the potholes are and make sure we don't hit them?

At most levels Graham was a product of the middle of the twentieth century's vision for evangelicalism that saw a deep renewal of evangelism and crusades and a very particular strain of saving souls as the Christian work of the day. But a story I read a few years ago still genuinely haunts me. And maybe it's because I travel and speak for a living and am gone from time to time traveling to churches and such.

Journalist William Martin did a deep dive on the family, including interviews with many of Graham's children, in an article titled "Divorce, Drugs, Drinking: Billy Graham's Children and Their Absent Father." One thing that stuck out to me profoundly was how much and how obviously the mission of saving souls and preaching took precedence over the team. Family was almost seen as a hurdle or hindrance to the "real work." To the point where Graham didn't even recognize his own kid when she was young because he had been gone so long.

The journalist noted, "Once, when Ruth [Graham's wife] brought Anne [his oldest daughter] to a crusade and let her surprise her father while he was talking on the telephone, he stared at the toddler with a blank look, not recognizing his own daughter." A few years later, his son saw him coming home and with a puzzled look asked, "Who is he?"

In one of the more painful parts of the article, his daughter Ruth, who endured four divorces, recalls bringing up the possibility of her first divorce with her dad. And Graham told her it would hurt millions of evangelical Christians who looked to his ministry and their family for inspiration.

She went on to recall, "I saw how important the ministry was to him—and how little the family was."[1]

And this isn't to come down on someone like Billy Graham. In fact, in one poignant part of the interview, Gigi, another of the Graham kids, noted her father's struggle with being pulled in so many different directions. Talking about how her father rarely disciplined her, she mentioned it was because one time when he did, she yelled back, "Some dad you are! You go away and leave us all the time!" And she said, "Immediately his eyes filled with tears. It just broke my heart. That whole scene was always a part of my memory bank after that."

Even Billy himself, when reflecting on his life in his

memoirs, said, "I know my absence had repercussions on my kids' lives."

As I became fascinated with the story of Graham and his legacy and family, I came across another interview—only eight minutes on YouTube—with his daughter Ruth, titled "Ruth Graham: Forgiving My Father." I'd suggest you put down this book and go watch that YouTube clip. What I love most is the complexity and tenderness and grace with which she walks through this problem with the interviewer.

She loves her dad. She is thankful for her dad. She praises God for her dad and the global work he did. But she also wants to pass on wisdom and knowledge of what she has learned. She said, "I had to forgive my father for a sense of abandonment as he traveled so much. I wanted a daddy to teach me how to ride a bike. To tuck me in bed at night."

She even noted that after decades of reflection she came to realize her many divorces could almost be directly traced back to her father's absence. "I had abandonment issues," she said. "And I was looking for security. And I would have told you Jesus was my security. But deep down where we keep our secrets that wasn't true. I was looking for a man to make me feel secure. So finally after the fourth marriage, I said what in the world is going on?"

The interviewer asked, "Do you think it's missing the mark for preachers to be gone so much when they have young children?"

"I do."[2]

And this is where we have to ask the really hard questions. Because we have been formed for decades in the West by a church that says there are two buckets, not one.

There is the ministry bucket.

And there is the family bucket.

These should not touch. Should not overlap.

And without saying so directly, the ministry bucket is considered to be much more important.

So you have a generation of fathers who dragged their families kicking and screaming around the globe to be on the mission field, when their wives and children might not have wanted any part in it.

But there is an equal, if not more pervasive, vision that swings the other way.

We call this one "Family *as* Mission." This is when families accidentally make the family itself the mission.

You see this a lot in homeschool and church communities, where, sadly, making a cute, nice, perfect moral family becomes the goal instead of reigning and ruling and building and bringing God's kingdom here on earth as it is in heaven *through* your family's talents and wirings and giftings.

In fact, this is very specifically the repeated place of indictment God has for the nation of Israel. They were blessed *to be a blessing.* Yet it's clear they went insular. They turned inward, when they were meant to be a conduit.

The minute you are building up your family team just to have a strong family team is the minute you are doing it wrong. When family becomes an idol, when we get our value and worth from how our family looks, acts, and presents to the world, and that becomes our entire focus, we can be crushed under the weight of expectation.

And here's the sad truth: that way of living is so tiny. We were created for grandeur and adventure and mission and huge vision, not making sure our kids say please and thank you and are liked by everyone in the church.

Now, one caveat I'd add: in the early years (think toddler and elementary years) it can *look* like the family is the mission, when instead it's just what we call a "training season." Meaning, during the first five to seven years, it is really helpful to not be running "on mission." The team needs to be built and trained and cohesive and powerful relationally first.

Then there is the third bucket, which is the one that comes from God's original design. It's the one most of us have such a hard time with, and that is "Family *on* Mission."

Not family *and* mission, not family *as* mission, but family *on* mission.

A family on mission embraces the truth that God wants them to work together as a team to accomplish what cannot be done alone. They know that they are a collective of strengths and wirings and giftings brought together to fulfill his mission on earth.

And that's God's vision, so let's get super practical using the example of our family. But before we get to ways Alyssa and I have tried to experiment going against that tide and the things we've changed, I want to drill down a little deeper and ask why.

If we don't deal with the why, we will continue to act like zombies living a reality we don't want but aren't even aware of. And in my reflections over the past few years, and after talking about this specific topic with hundreds of parents in our community in person and online, I've come to the conclusion it's really only about two things:

Money.

And purpose.

We will sacrifice our family on either the altar of "but I have to work to provide for us" or the altar of "I'm doing big things for God."

But both of those are deeply misguided.

MONEY

I don't want to make light of this one. I'm not talking about someone who is money hungry or whose affections have been entangled with the pursuit of more stuff and more wealth and more money so much so that it has become all consuming— though that can happen, and you have to always ask yourself if those tentacles have wrapped around you so tightly that you can't get free.

I'm referring to many folks I know for whom money is about survival.

Too much debt, so then too much work, and all of a sudden we are fifty years old and finally reaching some semblance of normalcy and financial health and our kids are nowhere to be found. They're getting married in a different state with no real connection to us because during the years that counted we were working instead of building relationships.

Now, this was out of necessity, and there are so many factors out of our control. But here's something we absolutely have to wrestle with: Would your kids have preferred a lifestyle with less stuff, fewer trips, one less car, a smaller house, fewer clothes, not as many electronics, and on and on, if it meant you were around more?

Basically, we work super hard to provide a lifestyle that our kids don't even want. *We want it.* But our kids don't want a lifestyle; they want us.

And there are still absolutely times when we are just scraping by and working hard and not having all the time we want with the kids, but my question is, is that your goal? Is that your direction? Is that your heart? Because that's what matters most.

And that's something my mom modeled better than anyone I know.

There were seasons when she worked three jobs. That plus my supercompetitive select baseball schedule made it so our schedules were pretty complex and insane. There were times we didn't know where we'd get food. There were plenty of times when school shopping was happening at Goodwill and garage sales. And on and on. And guess what? I didn't really care. Because my mom was so good at making us feel like a *team*.

She never missed a baseball game. (I mean literally, and I counted at least one thousand games in my life.) We went on road trips and camped all the time. We were together. And even though we truly were just trying to survive, she never let the pressure of getting more stuff or having nice things or whatnot crush us or take her away more.

And my favorite part? My mom was okay with making a radical decision sometimes.

If that meant picking up and moving across the state to a different city because it was better for us and our lifestyle, she didn't hesitate to move. And it's funny because the common story is the opposite, right—most people move across the country for a *bigger and better* job that will put even more pressure on them. Rarely do we move across the country to save more, pare down more, lean into simplicity, and have more time together as a family.

So we as parents have to wrestle with whether money and work conversations are more about us than the kids. Because you won't find a kid who says, "Yeah, I wish my dad and mom were gone a little longer so we can have a few nicer things or keep up a lifestyle that is already unsustainable."

PURPOSE

Another landmine we can step on is making a work decision or lifestyle choice based on the purpose it will give us. This is the category I'd put Billy Graham into. The family was sacrificed for the "mission" without realizing that the mission, once you are married and have kids, I'd argue, is *never* solitary. God doesn't give individual missions to teams.

Now, let me be clear: I don't mean the family does everything together, never leaves each other's sides, or has to always function as a unit. That's oversimplified. Too much of a caricature. In any team, the members have different assignments. But all of it is under the umbrella of the collective mission.

An ambassador for the United States has a different assignment than the president of the United States. But the mission is the same: to represent and further the goals of the collective Union. They are different teammates with different assignments on one team chasing one mission.

But when the toxin of individualism seeps into your bloodstream, you begin to make choices that are best for you but not best for the team. And while we celebrate that in families for some reason, you know what we call that in team sports?

A cancer.

Literally, that's the word I heard growing up on every team. They talk about it on SportsCenter. You'll hear it in coaching seminars. If an individual acts as though his purpose is more important than the team, we call that person a cancer on the team.

The player who cares more about his stats, getting the shot, getting the opportunity, or getting the MVP at the end of the year—we know what that person is like. And none of us want to be him.

Yet that's exactly what most of us do in family settings, even though in any other genre of teams—business, sports, military—we honor a person who submits and serves the mission of the team.

———

There is an interesting shift currently happening in our culture around this idea of individual purpose. When individual purpose becomes more important than a collective team mission, what you essentially do is create winners and losers.

The marriage and the family basically engage in a tug-of-war for who gets to achieve their purpose and goals and who has to put theirs on the back burner.

The horrible part of that truth is that the winner is almost always the dad, and the loser is almost always the mom. And if you add in distorted bad evangelical theology, that only compounds the problem—isn't it the wife's job to stay at home and drown and do everything that an entire corporate generational family (grandparents, nieces, household employees, and so on) used to help the family do a hundred years ago? No, it isn't.

In the nuclear family ideal, the mom's job has only gotten harder—every shift of going more and more into isolation has basically meant less and less help for the mother. And not to mention, she doesn't even have other adults in the home to talk to about these things. So American and evangelical motherhood in my opinion is not only the hardest and most impossible work, it is also the most lonely and isolated. And impossible work plus impossible loneliness? Devastating cocktail.

Unfortunately, the church often aligns with this view. The sad reality about most teaching and preaching from the evangelical world is that it's not trying to take us back to the ancient world of the Scriptures; as we talked about earlier, it's trying to take us back to 1950.

I like how Wendell Berry put it in his profound essay "Feminism, the Body, and Machine" (the only essay I make sure to read at the start of every year. It's that good). He flipped the script and asked,

> How . . . can women improve themselves by submitting to the same specialization, degradation, trivialization, and tyrannization of work that men have submitted to? And that question is made legitimate by another: How have men improved themselves by submitting to it? The answer is that men have not, and women cannot, improve themselves by submitting to it.[3]

The truth is, while men have submitted to that form of work, did you know it wasn't something at first consented to and, in fact, was met with deep resistance by men when they were called out of the home at the turn of the twentieth century?

And the mom is the one who loses. She picks up the slack at the expense of her own sanity and flourishing and well-being for the sake of the husband to find fulfillment outside of the home. And both secular and religious circles have supported this framework. The mom bears the brunt of everyone's needs and finds no fulfillment or satisfaction for herself. Her only state is burnout.

Then secular culture steps in and says, "No! You're a girl boss and *deserve* to fly just like your husband." Which, like many harmful ideas, is true but is resting on the wrong foundation.

Because who almost always loses in that scenario?

The kids.

If individual fulfillment and purpose-finding outside of the team is the goal, then hear me, there is *always* a loser. It's an endless game of tug-of-war. And who loses in tug-of-war? The weakest ones—in this case, the children.

But teams operate in the exact opposite way. Teams make decisions *together.* And then teams make decisions that serve *everyone.* And teams make calls where *everyone* flourishes.

Are there small moments of mutual sacrifice on teams? Of course. But those are made with the family mission in mind, building something greater or bigger. The sacrifices aren't about allowing one individual to repeatedly get what they want over and above everyone else.

So does your family have a bigger story? Is it being taken further? Does your team have a mission worth collectively sacrificing for?

Here's the best way to do a quick assessment to find out if you're a team or not: ask yourself if all your assets are being deployed.

What do I mean by that?

Your family, right now, in this moment, has tons of assets—and they should be written down somewhere, like on the Family Scouting Report. You might have particular leadership skills that no one else in the family does. Your spouse might have operational giftings and vision capabilities no one else has. Your oldest kid might be supersensitive emotionally and able to sense people's difficulties and know how to empathize or comfort them more than most. Your youngest kid might have a brilliant mind for solving problems.

So why then are they sitting on the bench waiting and are never called into the game?

Or why are you or they allowed to let those skills and assets be deployed at their work and school, but they are never activated at home? The truth is, family and home should get the best of everyone's talents and skills, before work or school or anything else does.

And that's what a true marital team is about—the husband's job is to release the wife's strongest assets into the world and their home with force and power. And the wife is to help unleash her husband's best giftings and talents in the same way.

Teams release and unleash the maximum potential of their team members. And you'll be shocked when that's happening to see how much more purpose you find in the home than outside of it.

If you work outside the home, make sure your identity and force of purpose are coming from the home and the team. Because if you're setting out to discover it somewhere else, destruction is all you will find.

And let me say it again, just so there is no room for misinterpretation: I am not saying working from home is best. I know plenty of awesome fathers who lead epic family teams and who are at the office six days a week, nine hours a day; and I know some work-from-home dads who have no vision and are abdicating their coaching responsibility. That's not the issue. The goal is to make home the orbiting force. Is home the center? Is home the headquarters? Is home the heartbeat of everything else?

Remember, this is a lifelong experiment in integration. You are not trying to solve this problem in a day or even a week or a year. You are experimenting with ideas, holding on to and building on to the ones that work and releasing the ones that don't.

The world is obsessed with disintegrating the family. Everything needs to be split up and divided. We divide school classrooms by twelve-month age periods (why?). We divide church classrooms by the same. We divide churches by adults and teens and kids. We divide extracurriculars by gender and age. On and on. There is barely any force in the world that wants your family to stay *integrated*. And so it's our job to ask hard questions and to look for ways strategically and thoughtfully to integrate our family.

What does *integrate* mean? The dictionary says "to form, coordinate, or blend into a functioning or unified whole."

Sounds like a team to me!

Alyssa and I have experimented with this intensely over the years, so we have a few ideas on how to integrate your family that might spark some thoughts for you.

The biggest and first one was regarding traveling for work. We asked, how can I integrate this with our team? So I started bringing a kid with me for special one-on-one dad time on work trips, and then I added an extra day for us to play and hang out. Before Kinsley was five years old, she'd probably logged a hundred thousand miles and been to Tennessee, California, Minnesota, Florida, Texas, and more with me.

But there was a slight risk with this plan. Because I wanted to hold this line, I started asking events to cover two plane tickets. And while I was terrified to make that request, you know what? So many were more than happy to fulfill it! I've heard other families say the same with their work or responsibilities. People love supporting these visions; it's just that our world doesn't operate on them, so it won't ever be the default. You have to ask for it and even at times fight for it. Sometimes the event couldn't afford the extra ticket, so I either had to decide we couldn't do it or pull from our savings or mileage points to make it happen.

Another angle we've taken on the travel and speaking front is giving our kids ownership over our job and calling. They absolutely light up when we allow them this kind of input.

What I mean by that is every trip or conference I get invited to gets tossed by the kids. I ask them if I should go, if they want to come, and how we can best be a team or go on a mission with this request. It's hilarious, and fascinating, to hear what comes out of their mouths. And it makes them feel like the work I do is our family's work, not just mine—which it is.

I heard from a friend who runs a nonprofit that his board actually decides every speaking trip for him. He doesn't even see the requests! The inquiry comes to them, and they consider it and ask questions and decide for him.

While I know of a handful of orgs that do this, I've never heard of a family that does. So Alyssa and I have decided that when the kids are a few years older, we are going to do this exact same thing. The email request or webform will go to Alyssa or one of the kids, not me. And once a month or so they'll have a family board meeting and decide which conferences or work trips I say yes to. I won't even see the request or know about it until it's already a yes and planned and scheduled. I know if I was a teenager, I would've *loved* that; not to mention all the real-life learning that teenagers rarely get in organizational leadership.

Another easy, yet hard on my spirit, rule I follow is that

when I run errands, one or all my kids come with me. Is this more work? Is it harder? Is it noisier? Yes. But it's made me slow down. You want a tool that'll curb hurry and hustle in your heart? Bring a toddler with you. And enjoy it.

I've come to believe that most of discipleship and teaching our kids comes in the everyday, not in the Sunday family devotionals. When you integrate your children into every aspect of your family, with the spirit of answering every one of their questions, you'll be surprised how much will be "caught" by the time they are out of the house.

To build a team mentality, it's imperative the kids know what mom and dad do. That it's explained. That it's brought in. The book *Iron John* by Robert Bly talks about the enormous shift that happened with fathers' work and the Industrial Revolution. He noted it was the first time in history when kids basically didn't know what their dad did for work.[4] And that's only gotten worse as we've gone from mostly blue collar work to white collar desk and computer work. This is another reason why we have decided to involve our kids so much in my travel and the decision making regarding my work. We want them to understand what we are doing and why. And we have done the same with Alyssa's work as well.

You can know you're achieving some success with this when you start seeing your kids mimic what you do. Like the time Kinsley came out of our room with my "preaching shoes" on and a Bible in her hand and got up on the table and started talking about Jesus. I remember her yelling, "Jeeezzzus is the best!" which I guess is basically what I say when I speak at conferences.

Or the time she was stapling a bunch of paper together with words and drawings on them, and when I asked her what she was doing, she said, "Writing a book like Mommy and Daddy."

I realized that only happens if you're constantly living life saying, "Hey, did you see that? Let me explain that a little," or integrating your kids into what you are doing and bringing them along with you.

Now, I am fully aware that my job is unique and not everyone has the privilege of working from home. So I surveyed our epic online Homeroom community—more than two thousand families, blended, divorced, old, young, with special needs, and more—and asked how they are integrating their families and giving touchpoints between work and home for their teams, and below are some great ideas. What surprised me was that some remembered what their own parents did that seemed so insignificant at the time but that transformed them and made them feel loved and part of a team.

Polly mentioned that when she was growing up her dad worked long hours and missed almost every dinner with the family. But he had gained just enough seniority that his company let him come in early to get a few hours in before the kids were up, and then he'd race home at 7:00 a.m. The two hours from 7:00 to 9:00 a.m. before he went back to his eighteen-hour day were crazy sacred, and she remembers the ritual of him making a big breakfast and talking to them for those first two hours of their day.

One mom mentioned that one day a week she and the kids meet dad for lunch outside with a little picnic. Another person hopped on this thread and said her husband works in a top-secret facility where family isn't even allowed inside the building so they do the picnic idea too.

One mom said she and her kids use a video messaging app, Marco Polo, to send highs and lows of their days to one another.

One military family wrote that it's imperative to them to have the kids "help pack Daddy's lunch, help put on his uniform patches every day, and group hugs and pray before they leave."

And this is one of my personal favorites: a dad who is an ER doctor picks a particular patient every night who the whole family prays for (without using identifying info). What vision to wrap your kids up in.

Another really creative one is a firefighter family that visits the station with the kids with snacks and support for the guys. And when it comes to holidays, the mom said they stopped celebrating on the exact day if dad had to work but instead made a saying, "Holidays are held by our family calendar," and holidays get scheduled on dad's closest day home.

In one family the husband is a videographer and works mostly at night, so a fun little treat the kids love is the morning after the dad has a gig or wedding, the family watches a few minutes of the raw footage he shot and he recaps the event for them.

A special needs teacher mom said she's constantly creating and making new resources for her special needs kids, so her daughter has been named chief resource tester and her husband is the chief laminator.

And I just loved the following from another one of our members in the community who is a military family:

> My husband has been in the military for fourteen years and we attend family events they put on, every graduation, etc. When he picks up a new rank or is honored in some way, he always includes our kids. Whether that's them pinning on his new rank, him introducing them to everyone he works with, etc. We also put a huge emphasis on staying together as a family whenever possible if work takes him away. For instance, he's in a school four hours away and we've visited him twice and he comes down every single weekend he can. He shows them that even when he's away they matter and he's trying to get back to us every chance he gets.
>
> The military gets a bad rep for family life which is fair in a lot of cases but there are also SO many opportunities to involve your family and make it a team effort. We visit him for lunch and he will show us his work space, he will teach them drill movements, FaceTimes them at work and shows them cool military stuff—just a bunch of things that help them feel like they are a part of it. And we always pray

for him. I'm sure I'm forgetting a bunch of things but that's what I can think of.

Another wife said her husband works sound for concerts and always brings one or two of the oldest to help and gives them a simple job.

Another one of my favorites:

My husband is a pilot with a private charter and is gone a lot and does not have a consistent schedule. We try and FaceTime a lot, and when dad is home they help him "plan" his trip. Getting fuel numbers, planning the trip and routes and airports. Whenever he's at a nearby airport for the night but can't come home (an hour or two drive) we will drive down and have lunch or mini hotel vacation night with him. Also anytime we see a plane in the sky we talk about dad and how we're a team and him working so hard allows me to be home fully with the kids.

And probably my personal favorite of the bunch, a woman shared about her father, a lawyer who worked intense and long hours, and how her mom would bring her siblings and her to the law office as much as possible and appropriate, and trained them to be useful so they served and helped the culture of the office. Reflecting on this time, she said she also had fond memories of "playing in the conference rooms when empty, making photo copies of our butts, and mooning passing cars on the streets from the glass elevator in the office."

I mean, if you're not taking pictures of your butts at your dad's law office, are you even integrating? Probably not.

NINE

Training and Vision

A few years ago Alyssa and I got invited on a tour of the headquarters of a worldwide home and renovation brand. We were invited by the assistant of the founders, Sarah. Sarah was showing us around, sharing stories, and letting us see behind the curtain of her bosses' empire. Also let me mention her bosses are very famous and ones you most likely know. To start the tour we drove around first seeing many of their properties while hearing fun and key elements of the story.

As we passed a big warehouse, she said, "That warehouse is ours too. We ship a lot out of there." I'm paraphrasing here, but she essentially said the business was exploding. I mean, out the walls, absurd, rocket-ship growth in a short amount of time, and recently they had needed more space, *fast*.

After just two weeks on the job, Sarah had been charged with finding a space for expansion. Talk about a whirlwind, jumping into a new job with that pace and those needs. And to make it even more fun, when they decided they needed another warehouse and a bigger one, the owners were across the country doing a big media tour while she was home in the southern states holding down the fort.

She got a text from one of her bosses while they were at the *Today Show*: "We need to get a warehouse. Right now."

She said, "Okay, I'll go research some options and send them to you."

He said, "No. I want you to go buy us a warehouse. I trust you. You know what we need, and this is why I hired you. Let me know when it's done."

She was *stunned*. Then almost paralyzed. Talk about pressure! A new job. New role. And tasked with buying a six-figure piece of real estate in a matter of days.

And guess what? She did it.

As she was telling us the story, she said it was crazy learning that sometimes people trust you more than you trust yourself. People believe you are more capable than you think you are. And on top of that, she said she knew deep down she had the freedom to fail given the support she had already experienced in her role.

Think about those words: *No. I believe in you. I trust you. You know what we need, and I know you can do this.*

I remember thinking, *That is exactly the dad I want to be. But could I be? Am I?*

It takes such a blend of relinquishing control, trust, and

coaching to be in a spot to say something like that and act like that. But it is possible. And so many of us parents don't even get in the same zip code as that philosophy.

And of course if people don't have the right tools, that kind of situation would not set someone up for success. But this story was obviously different. She said she *came alive*. And we know we would too. Why don't we let our kids have the same opportunity?

There's a magical matrix, I think: high demand coupled with high support.

High support, low demand creates coddled, baby-fied kids.

High demand, low support creates shameful, militaristic family cultures.

High support and high demand, though?

That's the absolute sweet spot. And that's how the best coaches we know act.

One of a coach's superpowers is knowing how to deliver constructive feedback. If a coach can nail this, it changes everything.[1] And usually when we fail in this regard, we and our players take a step backward. The feedback or "after action review" (as Navy SEALs call it) is sometimes even more important than the action or activity. The review is where the actual learning, the gluing of new values and systems and synapses, is happening.

What's your first guess on what you think is the most effective feedback or the most important variable? Most say quality of information. The technical specifics of the information given—do this and not that. And that *is* important. But that's not the most important.

A team of psychologists from Stanford, Yale, and Columbia (you know, decent schools) put some serious brain power and research behind discovering the most motivating feedback. They had middle school teachers assign essays to their classes, and after the assignments were given, the students were given different feedback.

Most of the feedback variables came back non-correlated, meaning they didn't see much of a difference between a few different types of feedback strategies. Except one.

In fact, there was one very specific feedback phrase and signal that boosted student performance so much they deemed it "magical." Students who received this very specific script performed significantly better than everyone else in their class—the study showed a 40 percent increase among white students and a 320 percent increase among black students.

And the feedback?

One sentence: "I'm giving you these comments because I have very high expectations and I know you can reach them."

That's it. Say those eighteen words, and a kid practically shoots through the roof.

Daniel Coyle reflected on the study by noting a few distinct, subtle, powerful layers in the eighteen words. Talking about the magic feedback he said, "They're powerful because they are not really feedback. They're a signal that creates something more powerful: a sense of belonging and connection."[2]

In fact, they contain three very specific signals:

1. You are a part of this group just like me.
2. This group is special, and because of that we have high standards.
3. I believe in you and that you can reach those standards.

The "I have very high expectations of you, because I believe you are capable of this and I will be here for you and alongside you the whole way" is the absolute heart of coaching. A coach is usually much more intensely focused on the you inside of you than you are. They see a future and a potential that you can't and are willing to help and assist in taking you there.

And the incredible jump specifically in African American students was because, as the study noted, "A large body of research attests to the subtle and not-so-subtle cues that send the message to minority students that they are seen as lacking and as not belonging in school. These include, among other things, harsher disciplinary actions, colder social treatment, and patronizing praise" and a level of "mistrust" develops that they've found the "magical feedback" profoundly counters.[3]

I still remember a profound moment I had in middle school in the principal's office when a few words he said buried deep into my soul and helped me along for years.

That particular meeting in the principal's office was to be my last. It was the meeting to inform me of my expulsion from the school. That office was very familiar to me, and I had almost made a habit of being in it. I had reached the end of the road this day—we both knew the school was no longer a good fit for me.

But the principal, let's call him Mr. Adleman, was a kind and incredibly empathetic man. Every time I was in his office, I felt seen, believed in, and understood, even though he also clearly had to administer consequences.

That day he looked at me as he was kicking me out of the school and said, "Jeff, I believe in you. When I look at you, I think of this story of an artist and a statue he was sculpting. A friend came by and saw a block of nothingness and jagged edges and marble and a bunch of dust and chisels and mess all over the ground and asked if he was going about it the right way. It just seemed so disorderly. To which the sculptor responded, 'For me to create something beautiful, there will be a mess on the floor to get there. There is beauty and goodness hiding in there.'"

Then he said, "Jeff, I think that's you. Maybe middle school will be your dust on the floor, but I see an incredibly talented and bright and kind young man in there who will come out if you keep working at it."

It's an understatement to say that his words rocked me. They would have for anyone because of his love and genuine empathy and belief, but you couple that with me not having a father figure around to tell me anything of that nature and you can imagine how much it shook me to have a powerful, kind, gentle man look me in the eyes and say those things.

Did I immediately turn my life around and get it together? No. I still rebelled at some level, and my mom would rip her hair out, wondering what was happening with her son. But I will tell you that a seed got planted in my heart that day, one that would come up every once in a while and has never been forgotten. A seed that held on and later was watered by different people and circumstances and became the foundation of change.

The more I've reflected on that moment and how pivotal it was for me, the more I realized that layered underneath the belief in me was the *high expectation*. I had no concept of my amounting to anything at that age. Like most kids acting out, I believed the opposite—*I'm not good enough, this is who I am*—and I was self-destructive.

But the seed or gold at the center of the belief in me was that an adult figure saw potential in me and called me to it!

And so ask yourself, are you parenting with enough vision for your kids? Do you imagine possibilities for them that they can't see? Or is your imagination stale with pictures that only line up with their worst self or current version?

Because that's one of the essences of what it means to be a coaching parent—you do the imaginative groundwork to see your kids in a new future and new creation possibilities that they themselves cannot see.

———

I've written about this before, so I won't belabor the point. But in the first year or two of our marriage, there was really only one fight we had. Over and over again.

Travel.

I needed to, and wanted to, for work. Alyssa hated it.

It was our main source of income. It brought me tons of joy to be able to fly all over and speak to and meet folks. But it stressed Alyssa out. She loves routine. Loves home. Loves repeatable days, and I don't. Could you have guessed that?

And this only got worse once we started having kids, and the stress became too much to travel all the time as a family. Hotel rooms. Feeding schedules. Sleeping schedules.

So we made the call to let me go and come back as quickly as I could. But "quickly as I could" is not that quick when your home base is a tiny speck in the middle of the Pacific Ocean, more than two thousand miles away from the nearest large land mass.

And so we'd be nicely into our routines of work and home life, when *bam*, I'd leave for five days and just blow it all apart. And Alyssa would start to resent my being gone. Not only did her job get way more difficult while I was gone, but she also had to deal with diapers and spit-up and obscurity, while her other half was exploring a cool new city, being able to have full meals without anyone crying, and more.

So she reached a breaking point and said, "I can't do this

anymore." (Pro tip: It's better to catch problems and try to solve them before they reach that phrase. We didn't.)

And so we started asking for help. I started calling other dads and husbands who traveled for work. We had other older couples over to pepper them with questions. And one stood out. I was chatting with another husband and father who had adult kids by then and asked him what we were doing wrong.

He said, "Do you and Alyssa have any type of shared language?"

Uh. I didn't even know what he meant, but I could guess my answer was no.

He said, "While it certainly won't solve the problem, beginning to talk and speak like a team will make a bigger difference than you think."

I was skeptical. My years of ingrained selfishness and patterns and headbutting—they'd evaporate just because we start talking like a team?

Looking back, I know he wasn't wrong. But this was during the early days of me thinking and reading about living as a team, and I wondered, *Could a small swap of language from "me" to "we" make that big of a difference?*

But I was willing to give it a try. So we began to change how we talked.

I'm not going to speak somewhere next weekend at that conference. *The team* is sending out an ambassador of Team Bethke to be a representative on their behalf, doing the family's work. Or another easy language change was the weekly habit of going around the dinner table, having the kids (and us) share ways we were thankful to be on the team this week, and how it helped us (found comfort, meant a lot to have that one sibling help me on a job, etc.).

And I kid you not, that type of shift—a language-only shift at some level, meaning I still traveled and still spoke—worked.

And what's interesting about a language shift is that it brings up myriad other issues. I realized once I started practicing talking like a team that I hadn't been really acting like I was part of a team.

It feels disingenuous to ask your wife what the best decision for the team is while wanting to do only what you want or care about most. I realized how that was only corroding our mission together. There is no such thing as a solo mission when you're a family team. There are solo ambassadorships, but the mission is the team's, and the team is the one doing the holding and the sending.

A few months into this language experiment, I was packing to get ready for my next trip. And since old habits die hard, I was already picturing the familiar ritual that happened every time I left. The kids crying, Alyssa trying to hold it in, and the weight of it all.

But right before walking out the door, I called "huddle up," and we all got down on the floor and said our goodbyes. And our daughter, Kinsley—I think she was three at the time— started praying, "Jesus, I pway you help daddy as he pweeches for us." And the team sent me out with a "you got this!" look and hugs and prayers.

To say I cried on the way to the airport is an understatement. The Uber driver probably didn't know what to think.

But these were tears of joy, not stress or tension like before. Instead, I was overwhelmed. *Wow, this really works, and this is how it's supposed to be. We are Team Bethke.*

And you know what that does while I'm in those random cities? I get more excited to report back to the team. I tell them what I'm doing, what kind of work happened, what has been a win so far, and more, so they can count the successes with me.

And sometimes that's all it takes. In fact, I'd say that's the best place to start. Shifting words and language does more and means more than you think. And we've adapted it in so many ways now that both Alyssa and I are working parents. The kids and I have been able to do the same thing with Alyssa when she travels; we crowd around her at the breakfast table to give her a big cheer as she writes a hard chapter of her book; on and on.

Teams talk like teams.

Individuals talk like individuals.

What language does your home and family reflect?

"Once a Spur, always a Spur."[4]

That's a line from Steve Kerr, a famous coach who knows more than almost anyone about teams and winning and working together. He has eight NBA championship rings, playing for the famous Chicago Bulls, then the San Antonio Spurs, and then coaching the last NBA dynasty, the Golden State Warriors.

Yet you don't hear him saying, "Once a Bull, always a Bull." Even though that was one of the most accomplished teams in basketball history! But it's clear from history it was a team also riddled with strife, jealousy, and more—it wasn't fun or enjoyable. But the Spurs? That team was a lifelong family—created in bonds of love and sacrifice to one another.

FAMILY SPOTLIGHT

The Bradley Family

What do you do when you have all these pictures in your mind of what it means to be a family, but then they are pretty quickly stripped from you? That was a question Katie Bradley began to wrestle with when her husband wanted a divorce. With three little boys fully in her care, she had to scramble as life got turned upside down, and she had to learn and relearn a new way of life for their team. In a crisis, a team folds or gets stronger. Hers got stronger.

My inkling is that many who learn about the family teams concept think, *Our family can't look like that.* Shame is an evil monster, and it has no part or say in the team and story God wants you to tell. Within the reality you live in, God is with you and is unleashing a vision for you and your family and providing hope in the future if you accept him. And that vision and hope is catalyzed by intentional time to *think strategically about your family. Then experiment and iterate. Then keep doing what's working.* Katie has been a part of our Homeroom and Family Teams community for a few years and was always insightful and encouraging to the community, so I asked her a few questions.

She said, "For us, family teams, and being 'Team Bradley' (a phrase we use *a lot* in our house) really means that we're in this together. Our family core values unite us and remind us that we're not going it alone in life. My kids are still very young, but they're already understanding that we are able to do more when we work together. And that our team might be different from other teams, but we are still a team—and can rely on each other."

I think my favorite part is how Katie called the boys up to a level of expectation. She told them, "Our team needs you, Mommy needs you, and you have a role and contribution to help us achieve God's purpose in this season."

But as someone who was raised by a single mom myself, there are genuine and real difficulties—especially with boys—that can be easy places for disintegration to sneak in or seeds of team fraying to happen. I asked her about team rituals and rhythms and if there are any she's implemented specifically to keep connected to the boys. And she said without a doubt, nighttime blessings.

They do the usual special stuff like reading a story and she tucks them in, but she adds one small ritual at the end: "I put my hands on their heads and I say a blessing and praise over them. It usually is something like 'Jesus, thank you for making Cade so brave, and kind, and fiery. Shape those gifts in him, Lord, and let him know how much our team needs those traits in him.'"

Sometimes, she said, she'll look her boys right in the eye while her hands are on their head and repeat a blessing over them: "You are loved. You are known by the King of the universe, Jesus. You have purpose and a story. You are safe. You are righteous. You are an ambassador of light."

I mean, can you even imagine what that can do to a child's heart, night after night after night? One of the saddest things I think about our more secularized society is that we are the least blessed culture. We don't bless. We don't look into each other's eyes and speak innumerable life. We don't unleash the blessings God has allowed us to speak over others when he gave us the authority of heaven and earth in his resurrection.

I ended our conversation with Katie by asking what she would tell a new parent or family hearing some of these ideas for the first time. And I loved her answer.

"If I could tell someone hearing about Family Teams for the first time something, it'd be 'you don't have to do it all.' I think not every system or rhythm is for every family, and that's okay. Not everything is for the season of life you're in, and that's okay. But if you'll create some core family values, write them down, stick them on the wall, and look at them a lot and just lean into being a team . . . you'll be able to sort out which things help your specific family go in the right direction, and you can focus on just those things. And it'll make the world of a difference. It's helped my little family so much to say 'these are the very important things right now' and 'this is our end target,' anything that doesn't get us that direction doesn't stay."

TEN

Rhythms and Rest

September 29, 1929, was a historic Sunday. And not because it was a month before the Stock Market Crash of 1929, aka Black Tuesday.

It's because it was the last relaxed Sunday the citizens of the Soviet Union enjoyed for the next eleven years. Joseph Stalin, the tyrant of the Soviet government, believed Sundays were "a genuine threat to the whirr and hum of industrial progress." Sundays were a waste of time, and only stood in the way of world domination and progress, because the machines sat silent. Productivity was nonexistent, and people "retreated to the comforts thought to be contrary to the revolutionary ideal, like family life or religious practice."[1]

So the Sunday following September 29, a dramatic shift was put into place. Eighty percent of the workers were told to go to work, and the seven-day week was immediately replaced with the *nepreryvka*, or what's translated as a "continuous working week."

The Soviet economist Yuri Larin noted the reason: "The machines need never be idle."[2] And though we read that and are shocked and feel the abusiveness and toxicity of that rule, aren't we, in the West, functionally the same?

The machines never sleep.

But we'll get back to that in a minute.

The Soviet reshaping of the calendar sounds like one of those dystopian fiction books, yet it actually occurred. The days were stripped of all their meaning, and each of the five days was replaced with a color and symbol you were assigned to—the wheatsheaf, red star, hammer and sickle, book, and woolen military cap. The colors and symbols indicated your assignment and schedule. It is interesting that Stalin wasn't expecting every person to work every single day. He just wanted a rotation of people so there was never a collective day off. Something you wouldn't think would make much of a difference, right?

Long story short: it failed. Miserably.

Productivity actually fell. Families were disrupted beyond belief. And the most shocking result of all was it even proved damaging for the machines—even they could not run every day all hours, without failing. So eleven years later, a decree of the presidium of the Supreme Soviet reinstituted the collective seven-day cycle with shared days of work and rest.

An attempt to "hack the system" ended up hacking the

hearts, bodies, and families of Russia to pieces. But the Russians weren't the only ones who tried to adapt or alter the week for their own purposes. France did something very similar during the height of the Revolution—except instead of shortening the week, they lengthened it—sometimes to ten days.

But on top of the ten-day extension, they also tried to alter the calendar. The calendar still had twelve months, but they were composed of sets of three weeks of ten days each. This left more than five or six days at the end of the year that were declared "holidays in honor of the revolutionary working class."[3]

Days were then divided into ten hours each, with each hour constituting a hundred minutes and each minute constituting a hundred seconds. My favorite part of all of this "reinventing time" is that watchmakers attempted to compensate and change timepieces to suit the redefinitions.

And while the Soviet's goal was based in some ways in industrial practice, France's goal was singular—to destroy any semblance of religion. "Breaking the liturgical cycle was the precise idea" and to "not only destroy an old faith, but to supply a new one, which would be in conformity with the new age, to give a supreme significance to the rise of science, the growth of the State and the improvement of civilization."[4] The French leaders then even deemed the first year of the revolution as year one.

Spoiler alert—it also epically failed.[5]

As have every other society attempting to change the

seven-day rhythm. Today humanity consistently, across all regions and geographies, honors the seven-day week.

The week, on the surface, has no seemingly obvious anchor to make it true, like other rhythms of the day and the year. The day is obviously marked by day and night—a representation of the earth rotating one time on its axis. The month—not perfect, but in general—is a representation of the lunar cycle or synodic month, which is 29.5 days. The year—a full trip around the sun.

But the week? There doesn't seem to be a similar reason for why we live within it—nothing tied to the stars or moon or seasons that we know of. So why, without fail, has it been impossible for cultures to adopt anything other than a seven-day week?

For a long time the answer from scholars has simply been "because that's the way it's always been done, dating back to the ancient Babylonians, and it's too difficult to change." That is, until the scholar Franz Halberg didn't like that answer. He felt it wasn't empirically true.

Halberg was a research professor at the University of Minnesota and was dubbed "the father of chrono-biology"—an exciting new field, measuring and researching the biological rhythms we have in our bodies or in the world around us.

And one innate biological rhythm he and others have studied and found to be true over and over again?

The seven-day week.

It has outlasted all its competitors to the point it can't be chance, he said. Halberg and other researchers have noted a self-governing seven-day rhythm just as strongly as the daily and monthly and yearly rhythms we all agree on, in things like heartbeats, blood pressure, body temperature, acid content in the blood, neurotransmitters, and the stress-coping hormone cortisol. Even the common cold submits to the circaseptan rhythm (a week).[6]

The cadence of six days of work, one day of rest is, in Halberg's words, a tool of rest and repair. And we know that's what the twenty-four-hour cycle does, right? When we sleep, our bodies are repairing themselves. Cleaning out and clearing out, and doing the important work that often goes unnoticed but which completely enables us to function during the time when we are awake.

The week is the exact same thing on a grander scale. We work—then we rest, repair, and heal. Or, for most of us, *we don't*.

Well, except for a few groups.

Dan Buettner has dedicated most of his life and research to "reverse engineering longevity," asking why some people live so long and trying to determine how others can replicate their longevity. In his research he's found some very compelling patterns and traits that are obvious, like certain health and food decisions and exercise, all mostly found in places like Sardinia, Italy, and Okinawa, Japan.

But there is one group he found in the United States who has essentially a superpower. One that gives them an entire decade longer of life compared to everyone around them.

Seventh-day Adventists.

"They take the idea of Sabbath very seriously," he said. And it pays off. Who would've thought taking a true day of delight and blessing might make you live a little longer? Actually, a lot longer.

As he noted, "About 84 percent of health care dollars are spent because of bad food choices, inactivity and unmanaged stress, and they have these cultural ways of managing stress through their Sabbath."[7]

AN IDENTITY-SHAPING DAY

The town is small. One of those "everybody knows everybody" type of towns. Most days people are just going about their business. But one day a week things are different. It's practically a local holiday. Maybe Religious Observance Day would be a good name.

If it's Sunday, you could walk the streets of the hundred-thousand-person town and not see a car or person in sight because everyone is at church.

This particular church is located at 1265 Lombardi Avenue.

The home of the Green Bay Packers—Lambeau Field.

Green Bay is one of the smallest towns in the country to have a professional sports team. The stadium seats seventy thousand people. Only a hundred thousand people live in the town. You can do the math.

As one die-hard Packers-lover-turned-journalist said, "You could realistically walk down Main Street in Green Bay on a Sunday in the fall and not see any cars or people walking the street. Everyone is inside, usually with a group, watching the Packers."[8]

Also, there seems to be a different spirit in the air. People are doing things you'd never see on a Tuesday.

Imagine you're walking toward the stadium and you look to your left and your right and you're flanked by men without their shirts on. Their stomachs and chests are painted half green, half yellow. You spot a few kids with huge fake pieces of cheese on their head.

Moms and grandmas are decked out with football jerseys and gear.

The crowd is walking to the stadium chanting:

"Go, Pack, Go."

"Go, Pack, Go."

"Go, Pack, Go."

As you're walking, you also notice religious icons everywhere: statues of Saint Vince Lombardi.

Every street name you walk by is a memorial—Favre Street, Holmgren Way, Hutson Road—all famous players lionized via a street sign dedication.

As the journalist Jesse Motiff noted, "You don't become a fan, you're born one. . . . Knowledge is passed down from generation to generation. . . . Sundays during the fall and winter are spent doing one thing, watch the Packers."[9]

Oh, and the day before includes immense preparation. Huge grocery store runs are made for the tailgating. The body paint is bought and laid out. The jersey is cleaned. Tickets are printed. Excitement begins to bubble.

This is what Sabbath should be.

Everything the Packers game has, a true shabbat for your family should have.

But isn't it funny how we embrace one but buck the other?

We talk a lot about Sabbath. I mean, a lot. I've included a chapter on it in three of the last four books I've written— all with different angles and purposes—but a chapter on the Sabbath, nonetheless.

Not to mention, in interacting with thousands of families through countless emails and conferences and workshops the last few years, one huge question we get over and over again about building a family team is "Where do we start?"

And my answer is the same. Every time.

Sabbath. Craft a day of rest.

Or perfect a family dinner as an identity-shaping ritual, at least to start. It's a superpower. It will turn your family upside down immediately.

But when we suggest that, we get the very predictable responses.

"Well, it feels weird to block off that day for just our family. I don't think we can."

But you do it with football.

"Saying a blessing over the kids and lighting some candles? That feels like a funny ritual."

But you do it with football. (Well, lighting candles? Probably not so much—but a chant and pregame ritual? All the time!)

"Prepping and getting everything ready and going to the store to get everything we need? That sounds like a lot of work."

But you do it with football.

"Making it the high point of the week that we anticipate and look forward to and build toward? That seems like too much pressure."

But you do it with football.

Before we go further, though, let's chat about the week as a secret superpower for the family. And it really comes down to how you see time.

In the West
Leads to a Life of
Endless Doing

In the East
Leads to a Life of
Passive Existing

In the Bible
Leads to a Life of
Progressive Being

In my last book I wrote a lot about how we actually got our modern, Western concept of time. And how it has not always been that way. I won't rehash that here, but suffice it to say, we are made in the image of how we keep time. Our time is measured to the minute; our clocks tick at the milli-second. Everything is measured and optimized and meant to be efficient, and our hearts feel the same—constantly ticking, marching, bulleting us toward a future we can't seem to reach.

But a little-known fact is that our modern concept of time was driven by time being mostly relative to localities, and thus modern railroads and trains began to crash into each other. That was no good, so folks realized we needed to get our time standardized (and allow the trains to run on time, which is where we got that phrase). And what does this show? People could exist outside of standardized time—even though that's hard to believe today.

But the second image is another view of time. We see this in many Eastern cultures. And certainly in more ancient Eastern cultures. In fact, in his brilliant book *Gift of the Jews*, Thomas Cahill argues this was the only view of time before ancient desert nomad people who were following Yahweh brought into existence the concept of future, that we are going somewhere.[10]

What's beautiful about the biblical view of time, as seen in the last picture, is it's more of a spiral. The way to get to the future is by steadily repeating and living within cycles and rhythms.

Here's a test to see truly what vision of time you believe: When you quickly think about time and your life, do you essentially see it as one large timeline with a beginning, middle, and end? That was a concept quite foreign to the ancient writers of the Scriptures. Instead, they saw time as essentially daily, weekly, and seasonally (yearly) rhythms that they were called to steward and repeat.

This matters because whatever story we believe, we become. Whatever we chase, forms us.

If you believe life is essentially a race to the finish line with big milestone markers along the way, then you will spend most of your time creating and trying to attain these milestone markers.

I call this the bucket list family. (No, I'm not talking about the awesome YouTube family. Aren't they the best?!)

You'll concentrate on trying to create big moments but will subtly feel time running out and so you better hurry and capture all the value out of them before time disappears. This is why most Americans think that one vacation a year will save their family.

I'd be willing to bet the house that a family dinner or a weekly ritual with maybe a marital date night once a week or once a month will do way more to transform your marriage and family than a vacation ever can. The vacation at the end of the year cannot, under any circumstance, make up for all the missed opportunities or lack of family connection or bonding throughout the year.

Big trips are important, but they should be celebration trips, not "save our family" or "I've been working so hard, please let this make up for it" trips. Big difference. A weekly family focuses not on the finish line or bucket list items, but on weekly rhythms they can incrementally improve and optimize for meaning.

Because here's the thing: the bucket list family and the weekly family want the same thing: meaning.

One is the American vision of getting it; the other is more ancient.

One is chasing and grabbing for a certain type of life; the other is opening our hands and receiving the music we've been given and learning to dance.

This small, dramatic shift changed our own family drastically. As a default bucket list family, all we felt was pressure. Pressure to keep up. Pressure to think of something better. Pressure to not miss big moments.

But when we became a weekly family, the pressure was off. Who cares that Sabbath sucked and the kids cried and when I lit the candles we almost burned the house down?

We get to try again next week.

Who cares that we barely got to Wednesday without feeling tired and burned out and upset at each other?

We get to try again next week.

We said we'd have a date night but didn't plan well.

Who cares? We get to try again next week.

And here's the key—you need some mechanisms to assess and adapt, and get 1 percent better the next week.

This is why we do our Sunday Business Meeting practice. Alyssa and I get out the schedules, plan the week strategically, and ask a few very important questions: 1) How can we serve each other this week? 2) What didn't work last week that we need to change or alter or tweak? 3) How can we make sure to protect the most important things like date night, Sabbath, and intentional time with the kids? Though this practice is vitally important to look forward to the week and get on the same page, the thing that is actually more important is saying what didn't work the previous week and looking at how we can incrementally change something to try to get better.

Because life is just a collection of weeks.

Learn to have a good week, and you'll look back on a good life.

Learn to get better in small ways every seven days, and you'll grow in large ways over the years.

Nail a week, nail a lifetime.

See, living in a weekly rhythm treats the week like a gift to steward. To receive. To rest in.

All that you are, in one week.

I also think there's another important feature of the week. It's the optimal identity-shaping container.

Meaning, the week truly defines who you are.

There are some things you do or don't do in a day. It's too small. There are some things you do or don't do in a year. It's too big.

But a week? A week is where we truly let our identity live.

It's why you hear people say, "I work Monday through Friday," but no one says, "I work January through December."

A day is too short to optimize and perfect. Too much

pressure to nail the day, which is what you will hear from most motivational e-course Facebook ad personalities. "Own the day!" And there's merit to that. But it's too rah-rah and doesn't account for the ups and downs, and we can't possibly fit all we care about in one day. And a year? The opposite problem. Too big. Too much pressure of vision.

But the week? Just perfect.

Here's another way to put it that a mentor told me a few years ago.

"Jeff, if something doesn't show up in your week, you can say it's important to you but it's not. If it doesn't show up in your week, you don't care about it as much as you say."

Rocked.

I can say I value one-on-one time with the kids—but does it show up in my week?

I can say I value making sure we have a few intentional meals together as a family—but does it show up in my week?

I can say I value rest and renewal—but does it show up in my week?

I can say I value writing and creating—but does it show up in my week?

That's the gold standard. That's the test of value and importance and identity.

You only get to claim something as an identity and of importance if it shows up in your week.

And of course, there are exceptions. There are seasons where I don't write books for months on end. But I'm still a writer because there are plenty of weeks and months and even years where it shows up in my week.

But letting the week be the start and stop of importance absolutely crushes the unhelpful spirit of "Well, someday we will do that . . ." while also taking off the pressure of the day needing to be perfect and optimized. It's important to you? Learn to put it into your week.

And rest or a family holiday is the perfect place to start.

And it's where we started.

Why does it matter? Because what you're trying to do is create the high point of your family and week.

Everyone has a high point. Or zenith. Or climax.

When you think through your Sunday to Saturday this week right now, what immediately pops out as the high point you're looking forward to most?

Most people in the West tend to gravitate toward something with friends—the Friday-night meetup at the bar or restaurant after a long workweek, the Sunday pick-up basketball game with other dads. And of course all of these are fine and great.

But what if, just maybe, you could craft and create a day that had that spirit and power but for your team? What if the high point for the mom and the dad and the teenage daughter and the tween son was the Friday night dinner?

To us, that's our hope, and that's why we craft it in a certain way.

Sabbath is not a legalistic, worrisome practice. If you

are even asking yourself what you can and cannot do on the Sabbath, you've already missed the point. Stop asking that question. Start writing down things that bring you life and do more of that!

This is why we try to do what I heard one pastor call "pleasure stacking" on the Sabbath. Our biggest delights, our biggest pleasures, the things we love personally and corporately the most as a family—how can we continually stack those into that day? And it also has a cool delay of gratification for the kids.

No, you can't have ice cream before dinner tonight.

No, we can't watch a movie right now before naptime.

No, we can't do x, y, z . . .

But Friday night? *Let's do it all because God is good and it's time to party.*

We've noticed the power of anticipation. Work lights up because it's meaningful and not Groundhog Day. You know at the end of the week you will be refreshed and renewed.

We are good at relaxing in the West, but we are not good at renewing. Repairing. Putting back together. Filling. Delighting. Enjoying. Blessing.

And that's Sabbath. As a family it does a few specific things:

- It is the family's chance to resist the insane idolatry of work and productivity. It's a day to remind ourselves that we are not what we do and we are not what we have.
- It's an identity-shaping day, a high point or mini holiday for your last name.

- It's a generational ritual.
- It's a day of filling and rest.

And by the way, we get asked the question at Family Teams a lot that goes somewhere along the lines of "What if we have teens? What if there's a sports game that night? What if we can't get everyone together for our family?"

And I have two thoughts.

First, you have to seriously consider why everything in our culture is given precedence over family. It would be unheard of for our boss to say, "You need to show up at this time every day unless another commitment comes up. If something happens that you think is more important, then of course you can scrap your work commitment." Or for a sports coach to say, "See you at practice tomorrow! Well, unless something better comes up."

I really don't know why, but in our culture we almost *refuse* to hold the line for family events or family time.

Everything else always wins.

Sports win.
Friends win.
Church wins.
Ministry wins.
Busyness wins.

And we aren't saying you should have a family night every night. You shouldn't.

If you can't even hold the line for one night, one day a week, for a few hours as a family, do you really think anyone in the family would believe that family is actually important? Nothing in your life is supporting that idea if it's not shown.

If we continually show that family is the last priority and we only have special team time when there is nothing more important going on, well then, I think our kids will get the idea loud and clear that there is a lot that is more important.

And second, to those families with teens, turn the home and Sabbath dinner (or family night or whatever you call it) into an orbiting vacuum force that sucks everyone else in. Turn it into a night they can't refuse. Turn it into a time they want to invite their friends to, not leave.

And we've seen tons of families do this well in our Family Teams community.

Surprise! When you make a feast, laugh and play, and have a good time, people are attracted to that. Even teenagers. In fact, when I was that age I knew a full and big family table would've absolutely rocked my socks off. And it should.

Do people experience a taste of the kingdom of God when they sit at your table? They should.

Because at the end of the day, this is what a family should be doing. A family, enjoying good food and drink, sharing stories, and living into their identity through a shared meal is exactly what the kingdom is and what Jesus came to bring and show.

Jew and Gentile.

Male and female.

Rich and poor.

Black and white.

All sitting at a table. All feasting. All enjoying. All equal. All one in Jesus as the new family of God.

And that's why rest and family identity-shaping days are so important—that's the story you're telling. And that's why a day of rest, I think, should be not only personal but corporate. True rest is when we rest in each other.

Remember the Soviet story at the beginning of this chapter about eliminating the weekly calendar for eleven years?

You know what I found most interesting about their system? Technically, people in the five-day week had *more rest* than in the seven-day rhythm.

You got a day off every five days, not every seven.

Shouldn't that actually have been better? Wouldn't they actually have been better rested?

Why did it crush the entire country and morale and families and spirit, and why was it such a devastating fail of an experiment?

Because someone was always working. They eliminated shared corporate rest.

Every single person was assigned a different day of rest— even different from some of their family members. At any given time, twenty-four hours a day, five days a week, at least a handful of the population was working and the factories were running.

Isn't it funny, though, how in communist Russia this was a devastating experiment that literally crushed their economy and spirit and people, yet in the West, we willingly choose to basically do the same thing?

In fact, economists and historians argue that Russia's leadership specifically chose the fragmentation of families' rest schedule to purposely weaken families. Making family units less integrated may even have been a conscious part of the agenda. "Here, there was no common rest." Without it, it was easier for Soviet powers to divide and conquer.

Aligning the family schedule for shared days of identity and rest feels stuffy. Constricting. Not free. So we live lives of sporadic scheduling, taking a break only when we burn out, never rhythmically to fill ourselves or our family.

FAMILY SPOTLIGHT

The Pratt Family

FAMILY OLYMPICS

What do you do when you're really good at design, events, and community organizing?

Well, if you're Ian and Hannah Pratt, you use those gifts

and point them toward your family and start what they call Annual Family Camp.

What's Family Camp? Think of it as similar to a family reunion they help host, but with some seriously fun extras. Every single year they invite the whole extended family to this tiny cabin in the woods they have inherited.

Here's how it works. Each family unit (couple or single parent and their kids) is assigned their own color and family jacket. The jackets are a big deal, by the way—similar to a letterman's jacket, each family over the years earns and places patches on them. One of the main patches they get is the yearly patch everyone gets for participating in that year's shared project (one year the project was building a new switchback road from the cabin to the lake).

My favorite part? Each person is assigned an animal as their own personal symbol and icon within the family. In fact, Ian has mentioned this as his personal favorite, too, and what started as a fun "pick your animal" idea has now turned into a full-blown identity-shaping ritual where animals are picked based on traits and vision and blessings laid upon that kid. And when do you get your animal? During your coming-of-age ceremony, where the family lays hands, speaks life, and "crosses you over" into adulthood in the family, giving you a new identity. Talk about powerful!

And don't let the serious stuff fool you. There is also some serious competition! In fact, when everyone shows up there is an itinerary for the entire family accounting for every block of time over the three-day period. Competitions and races and relays—and one specific night set aside for identity speaking.

Ian said, "We want Family Camp to be a high point of the year, something that would build on itself year after year. So every year we compete as families for the coveted Family Trophy. And the winning family holds the trophy the entire next year (usually proudly displayed in their living room!) until the next one."

When I was chatting with him, he mentioned how needed that year's camp was, which was coming up in a few weeks.

"It's been a rough couple of years for several family members, lots of hard transitions, and some serious loss of identity for a few of us. So this year we are setting aside a whole day different from the games and Olympics and just an entire day where I'm trying to find some curriculum and exercises for us to collectively sharpen and dive deeper into our identities and encourage where we need encouragement. It doesn't come easy, this level of intentionality and commitment to family, but it's one of the most truly redemptive things we can do with our lives—and it allows us to carry forward the narrative for our family, knowing even the best is yet to come."

ELEVEN

Community Impact

You shall not go after other gods, the gods
of the peoples who are around you.

—DEUTERONOMY 6:14 ESV

Western families are built to consume. To have more. To make
it bigger. To spend more.

Here are just a few family statistics:

- There are on average more than 300,000 items in every
  American home.
- More than 25 percent of family homes that have two-
  car garages say they are too full to even park in them.
- An average American child has around 238 toys, yet
  only plays consistently with 12 daily.

- Three percent of the world's children live in the United States, yet they own 40 percent of the toys consumed and made globally.[1]

To home in on toys for a second, there is an obvious spike in consumption among children that started fifty or so years ago. Cultural historian Howard Chudacoff said this isn't a coincidence and that this dynamic coincides with a watershed moment in 1955. What happened in 1955?

The Mickey Mouse Club premiered and provided a mass-scale, entertainment-based marketing avenue for toymakers.[2] "Almost overnight . . . children's play became less focused on activities, and more on the things involved."

But this isn't a surprise. This is what factories do. They create a bunch of crap we mostly don't need, on a large and cheap scale, and then market it to us as if it's a necessity.

It's not.

But you know what is a necessity?

Food.

Feeding ourselves.

Nourishing our bodies.

And what provides the food?

Farms do. Farms are built for contribution, not consumption. They are built to contribute to the necessary needs of others and those around them. And that's what we want to do: feed others. We want to be a family that spends a lot of time working deeply and thoughtfully, bringing something into the world that actually feeds people. Their souls, stomachs, hearts, and minds.

And so we try our hardest to let contribution over consumption win out in every facet of our family's life.

Take finances. Because my mom and I ate dinners and had a roof over our heads because of many generous people, I wanted to do the same when I was older. Not to mention I think Jesus' theory of "it is more blessed to give than to receive"[3] is a true axiom more of us should stress test. So we set aside money every month that goes into a separate account, and its only purpose is to give it away.

A few months ago we were in a small group of friends, and one was honest and vulnerable and mentioned how their truck broke down and needed an expensive part. They were in a bind financially at the moment and asked if they could borrow a car or get some help. I asked how much it was. They said $600, and I said, "Done. It's yours."

On the ride home it was fun to chat with the kids about how our family resources are stewarded and used in a way we can deploy them that quickly to meet certain needs. Because at the end of the day, it's just a psychological trick, but it works. If we didn't put the money every month into the other account, we would still have the same amount (or maybe not!), but if a need arose we'd probably find a way to say we didn't have the money to help. But since it was earmarked and separated for such moments, it became an impulse give. And that's how you invert the culture's version of impulse buy. Use the same tactics and flip them on their heads.

And my favorite part? I've told the kids that the fund is our family's, not just Mom and Dad's. You want to help out that friend who mentioned they need some new shoes, or you overheard that conversation Mom had about a friend who lost their job and is struggling to pay rent and you think we should take it out of the fund? Done.

See, I'm convinced the reason our kids only consume and consume and consume is because we give them nothing better to do. How do I know this? Because I do it *literally*. What do I do when I'm bored? I eat. Because there's nothing better to do.

And we baby our kids and don't allow them to contribute or serve or give or be involved with large decisions, so how else would we expect them to do anything but eat and consume and absorb?

But if you give a kid a mission or something larger than their personal tastes and what feels good, it is no surprise it fuses the family more and more into a powerful team.

It's why just the other day my friend asked me to help him move. And I thought, *Hey, of course I can help. But wouldn't it be fun if the Bethkes helped, not just me?* And so I brought Kinsley with me. And was she the only person under thirty there? Yep. And did she seriously contribute and jump all in? She did. And it was a proud moment. And what struck me was that our team can work together and bless other people. Something about that gives a shared joy—noted by the high five she and I shared on the way home, with the added ice cream cone as a thanks for her help.

We constantly call our family "the Bethke board room"; Alyssa and I pretend we are the chairmen of the board, with our kids being representatives around the table, all tasked with contributing to the resources and distributing them as best as possible. And taking that mentality and including your kids changes everything!

One of the biggest scriptural principles linked to groups and teams and families is the concept of "blessed to be a blessing," which is a mantra we say a lot in our home. Abraham, one of the chief architects of this multigenerational family team vision, was blessed with the promise of a son, so that all the nations would be blessed.

It's like a stream. Have you ever seen water that comes in one way but has nowhere to go? There's a word for that. *Stagnant.* It pools up, begins to turn green, and stinks and smells and provides no value—in fact, it becomes a liability! That's a family oriented around consumption.

But a family oriented around contribution is a stream that receives blessing from God in one direction and then lets that *flow out of them* to the other side, providing life and nourishment and refreshment as a crystal-clear river to others.

And so, in many ways, even though we are six years into this family course correction toward God's idea, we are very much in its infancy. Whether your kids are adults and married and "moved on" or you just had your first child, it's never too late to lean into God's heart and vision. For starters, he's a God full of grace for the moment and allows us to always "start from now." The grace covers us and enables us today to take one more step toward him. And two, even if you are fifty years "late" in a project that's going to take five hundred years, then that's really not that late, is it? Think of your great-great-great-great-grandchildren and the legacy you want to leave—and that is where you are going and where God wants to take your family team.

In fact, some of the indigenous population already has this as their communal wisdom. Oren Leyons, chief of the Onondaga Nation, wrote: "We are looking ahead, as is one of the first mandates given us as chiefs, to make sure and to make every decision that we make relate to the welfare and well-being of the seventh generation to come. . . . What about the seventh generation? Where are you taking them? What will they have?"[4]

Good questions to think on, and good questions to leave with as you begin to build your family team!

Acknowledgments

One of my favorite parts of writing a book is looking back after it's published and realizing all the hands that had a part in helping nudge it over the finish line so that you could be reading it right now! It takes a team of various skill sets, and a few years of energy and work, to bring it to fruition. And this book is no different!

To Team Bethke—you guys are my first listening ears, places to bounce ideas off of, critics and encouragers, and I wouldn't want it any other way. I'm beyond blessed that God would allow me to be on a team with you all! Alyssa, you make me better every day and are such a gift. And to the squad (Kinsley, Kannon, and Lucy), I love you guys so much and am so thankful for all you teach me! What a gift to be your dad.

Curtis and Mike (and the Yates team!)—it's crazy to think we are right on the cusp of ten years of doing this dance together. There really isn't a better team out there, and you guys have gone from business partners to friends to family.

Thanks for believing in me back in 2012 and giving this guy a shot to write a few words on a page and thinking folks would be interested!

Angela—I always tell people when they say they love my writing, what they really mean is they love my messy ideas plus your magic touch. You have such a gift for helping me get those ideas into a more beautiful and compelling form. You are the chief idea shepherder and it's crazy to think this is our fifth book working together! Alyssa and I appreciate you so much.

Nelson Books squad—when I say I've got the best team in the business, I MEAN it. Y'all are so gifted, kind, gracious, and incredible. You guys took a shot on me as a twenty-two-year-old and I still don't know why, but I do know I'm GRATEFUL. To Tim, Jenny, Janene, Karen, Sara, Jamie, Rachel, and Kathie, you guys are the best!

To Mom—the first place I learned how to be a family team was with you. You had to fight for US so much, and you taught me so many things in that regard. Thanks for always being there for me and being such a gift to me. I wouldn't be who I am today without you! Love you!

To our Maui Ohana—as I wrote this book I was constantly overwhelmed with gratitude, thinking about how special our community is. You know who you are. But it's such a gift to know we have so many family teams building legacy and families who will go out and push back the darkness in their lives, jobs, and marriages.

Notes

CHAPTER 1: A RECENT HISTORY OF EVENTS

1. Claudio Sanchez, "Poverty, Dropouts, Pregnancy, Suicide: What the Numbers Say About Fatherless Kids," NPR, June 18, 2017, www.npr.org/sections/ed/2017/06/18/533062607/poverty -dropouts-pregnancy-suicide-what-the-numbers-say-about -fatherless-kids.
2. Sanchez, "Poverty, Dropouts, Pregnancy, Suicide."
3. Asher and Lyric Fergusson, "The Best Countries to Raise a Family in 2020," Asher & Lyric, July 24, 2020, https://www .asherfergusson.com/raising-a-family-index/.
4. Fergusson, "Best Countries."
5. "Lonely Lives: Alarming Number of Seniors Go Entire Week Without Talking to Anyone," studyfinds.org, September 7, 2019, https://studyfinds.org/lonely-lives-alarming-number-of -seniors-go-entire-week-without-talking-to-anyone/.
6. Emiko Jozuka, "Inside the Japanese Town That Pays Cash for Kids," CNN, February 3, 2019, https://www.cnn.com/2018/12/27 /health/japan-fertility-birth-rate-children-intl/index.html.

CHAPTER 2: THE MYTH OF THE NUCLEAR FAMILY

1. David Brooks, "The Nuclear Family Was a Mistake," *Atlantic*, March 2020, https://www.theatlantic.com/magazine/archive/2020/03/the-nuclear-family-was-a-mistake/605536/.

2. Wade Davis, "The Unraveling of America," *Rolling Stone*, August 6, 2020, https://www.rollingstone.com/politics/political-commentary/covid-19-end-of-american-era-wade-davis-1038206/.

3. Franchise Opportunities, "A Map of the Average Child Care Costs by State," businessbroker.net, April 12, 2018, https://www.businessbroker.net/blog/good-info-for-new-buyers-and-sellers/average-child-care-costs-state-map.

4. Lawrence Mishel, Elise Gould, and Josh Bivens, "Wage Stagnation in Nine Charts," Economic Policy Institute, January 6, 2015, https://www.epi.org/publication/charting-wage-stagnation/.

5. Wendell Berry, "Feminism, the Body, and the Machine," in *What Are People For?*, https://religioustech.org/wp-content/uploads/2019/09/Berry-Wendell-Feminism-the-Body-and-the-Machine.pdf.

6. Alan C. Carlson, "Atomistic v. Domestic Family," *Tom Shakely* (blog), June 17, 2018, https://tomshakely.com/2018/atomistic-v-domestic-family/.

7. Scott Hahn, *First Comes Love* (New York: Doubleday, 2002), 21.

8. Hahn, *First Comes Love*, 22.

9. Hahn, *First Comes Love*.

10. Hahn, *First Comes Love*.

11. Derek Thompson, "The Future of the City Is Childless," *Atlantic*, July 18, 2019, https://www.theatlantic.com/ideas/archive/2019/07/where-have-all-the-children-gone/594133/.

12. Thompson, "Future of the City."

13. "Does the Future of Humanity Pass by Way of the Family,"

Familiaris Consortio, 75, https://www.johnpaulii.edu/files
/20110414_J.Schindler.future_of_humanity.pdf.

CHAPTER 3: SEARS SHAPED HOW WE THINK ABOUT FAMILY

1. "The House That Came in the Mail," 99% Invisible,
   episode 323, produced by Joe Roseberg, September 11, 2018,
   https://99percentinvisible.org/episode/the-house-that-came-in
   -the-mail/.
2. "The House That Came in the Mail."
3. Patrick Sisson, "How Sears Kit Homes Changed Housing,"
   curbed.com, October 16, 2018, https://archive.curbed.com
   /2018/10/16/17984616/sears-catalog-home-kit-mail-order
   -prefab-housing.
4. Logan Paul, "Erich Weinstein Is the Smartest Man in the
   World," Implausive (podcast), episode 96, July 3, 2019, https://
   podtail.com/en/podcast/implausive-with-logan-paul/eric
   -weinstein-is-the-smartest-man-in-the-world-im/.
5. Markus Krajewski, "The Great Lightbulb Conspiracy," *IEEE
   Spectrum*, September 24, 2014, https://spectrum.ieee.org/tech
   -history/dawn-of-electronics/the-great-lightbulb-conspiracy.
6. Acts 7:32.
7. Joe Pinsker, "How Much Inheritance Is Too Much?" *Atlantic*,
   October 25, 2019, https://www.theatlantic.com/family/archive
   /2019/10/big-inheritances-how-much-to-leave/600703/.
8. Amanda Harding, "The Real Reason Bill Gates' Children
   Won't Inherit Much of His Fortune," cheatsheet.com,
   February 17, 2019, https://www.cheatsheet.com/entertainment
   /the-real-reason-bill-gates-children-wont-inherit-much-of
   -his-fortune.html/.

CHAPTER 4: THE ORIGINAL FAMILY BLUEPRINT

1. Matthew 19:4.

2. Genesis 1:27 NET.

3. Genesis 2:15.

4. Matthew 28:18–19.

CHAPTER 5: WHY TEAMS ARE THE WAY TO GO

1. Anders Greenspan, "Book Review: *History Is Bunk*: Assembling the Past at Henry Ford's Greenfield Village," *Public Historian* 37, no. 1 (February 2915): 129–30, https://online.ucpress.edu /tph/article-abstract/37/1/129/90647/Book-Review-History -is-Bunk-Assembling-the-Past-at?redirectedFrom=fulltext.

2. "Exploring the Origins of Greenfield Village," The Henry Ford, March 31, 2012, www.thehenryford.org/explore/blog /exploring-the-origins-of-greenfield-village.

3. Deuteronomy 6:18 ESV.

4. Jabari Young, "Parker-Popovich Relationship Resembles What Spurs Coach Had with Duncan," February 13, 2017, https:// www.expressnews.com/sports/spurs/article/Parker-Popovich -relationship-resembles-what-Spurs-10929485.php.

5. Peter Skillman, "The Design Challenge: Also Called Spaghetti Tower," https://medium.com, April 14, 2019, medium.com /@peterskillman/the-design-challenge-also-called-spaghetti -tower-cda62685e15b.

6. Skillman, "Design Challenge."

7. Daniel Coyle, "An Excerpt from *The Culture Code*," accessed April 7, 2021, http://danielcoyle.com/excerpt-culture-code/.

CHAPTER 6: DRAFTING YOUR TEAM

1. Iassen Donov, "Our Fallen Heroes: Nate Hardy," *SOFREP*, November 13, 2012, https://sofrep.com/news/nate-hardy-seal/.

2. Joshua Rothman, "Big Data Comes to the Office," *New Yorker*, June 3, 2014, https://www.newyorker.com/books/joshua -rothman/big-data-comes-to-the-office.

3. Alex Pentland, "The New Science of Building Great Teams," *Harvard Business Review*, April 2012, https://hbr.org/2012/04 /the-new-science-of-building-great-teams.

4. Rothman, "Big Data Comes to the Office."

5. Rothman, "Big Data Comes to the Office."

6. Pentland, "New Science."

CHAPTER 7: SAME ENEMY, SAME GOAL

1. Liz Welch, "Shake Shack's Danny Meyer: 'I Was Completely Convinced I Was an Imposter,'" *Inc.* magazine, May 2015, https://www.inc.com/magazine/201505/liz-welch/danny-meyer -shake-shack-icons-of-entrepreneurship.html.

2. Interview with Daniel Coyle, "Cracking the Culture Code," *The Growth Show* (podcast), December 2018, https://podcasts.apple .com/nz/podcast/cracking-the-culture-code/id963131164?i =1000425645614.

3. Carolyn Cutrone, "Danny Meyer to 'Treps: Put Your Employees First, Customers Will Follow," *Inc.* magazine, January 28, 2014, https://www.inc.com/carolyn-cutrone /danny-meyer-speaks-at-inc-business-owners-council.html.

4. Ann Graham, "Danny Meyer's Recipe for Success," *Strategy + Business*, June 20, 2018, https://www.strategy-business.com /article/Danny-Meyers-Recipe-for-Success?gko=3eff4.

5. Twila Van Leer, "2 Pioneer Stories That Recall Tragedy, Triumph," deseret.com, October 18, 2017, https://www.deseret.com/2017/10 /18/20621752/twila-van-leer-2-pioneer-stories-that-recall-tragedy -triumph#sunset-through-a-wagon-wheel-on-the-second-day-of -the-farmington-utah-south-stake-pioneer-trek-held-near -evanston-wyoming-but-on-the-utah-side-of-the-border-june -26-2008-ravell-call-deseret-news; "Mary Goble: Walking to Zion," Elbow Room: The West, http://bsmudde.weebly .com/uploads/5/8/7/9/58794057/morman_and_ca_trail.pdf.

6. Jeffrey Marx, *Season of Life* (New York: Simon & Schuster, 2004), 3.

7. Sebastian Junger, *Tribe: On Homecoming and Belonging* (New York: Twelve, 2016).

8. Gordon Neufeld and Gabor Maté, *Hold onto Your Kids* (New York: Ballantine, 2014).

9. Zara Zareen, "What Are the Warning Signs of an Emotional Affair," medium.com, November 19, 2019, https://medium.com /@zara.zareen/what-are-the-warning-signs-of-an-emotional -affair-80537616d7a6.

10. Neufeld and Maté, *Hold onto Your Kids*.

11. Neufeld and Maté, *Hold onto Your Kids*.

12. Marx, *Season of Life*.

CHAPTER 8: FAMILY ON MISSION

1. William Martin, "Divorce, Drugs, Drinking: Billy Graham's Children and Their Absent Father," *Washington Post*, February 21, 2018, https://www.washingtonpost.com/news /acts-of-faith/wp/2018/02/21/divorce-drugs-drinking-billy -grahams-children-and-their-absent-father/.

2. "Ruth Graham: Forgiving My Father," November 13, 2019, YouTube, https://www.youtube.com/watch?v=z49nBB0BW-o.

3. Wendell Berry, "Feminism, the Body, and the Machine," *What Are People For*, accessed April 11, 2011, https://religioustech .org/wp-content/uploads/2019/09/Berry-Wendell-Feminism -the-Body-and-the-Machine.pdf.

4. Robert Bly, *Iron John: A Book About Men* (Boston: Da Capo Press, 1990, 2004).

CHAPTER 9: TRAINING AND VISION

1. Daniel Coyle, "The Simple Phrase That Increases Effort 40%," *Daniel Coyle* (blog), December 13, 2013, http://danielcoyle .com/2013/12/13/the-simple-phrase-that-increases-effort-40/.

2. Coyle, "Simple Phrase."
3. David Scott Yeager et al. "Breaking the Cycle of Mistrust: Wise Interventions to Provide Critical Feedback Across the Racial Divide," *Journal of Experimental Psychology: General*, 143: 2 (804–24), https://www.apa.org/pubs/journals/releases/xge-a0033906.pdf.
4. Scott Ostler, "In San Antonio the Spurs Are Like Family," *San Francisco Chronicle*, April 21, 2018, https://www.sfchronicle.com/sports/ostler/article/In-San-Antonio-the-Spurs-are-like-family-12854207.php.

CHAPTER 10: RHYTHMS AND REST

1. Natasha Frost, "For 11 Years, the Soviet Union Had No Weekends," history.com, August 30, 2018, https://www.history.com/news/soviet-union-stalin-weekend-labor-policy.
2. Frost, "Soviet Union Had No Weekends."
3. [[Need Source]]
4. Ed Simon, "Why the French Revolution's 'Rational' Calendar Wasn't," *JSTOR Daily*, May 23, 2018, https://daily.jstor.org/why-the-french-revolutions-rational-calendar-wasnt/.
5. Simon, "French Revolution's 'Rational' Calendar."
6. Alain Reinberg, Laurence Dejardin, Michael H. Smolensky, and Yvan Touitou, "Seven-Day Human Biological Rhythms," *Journal of Biological and Medical Rhythm Research* 34: 2 (2017), abstract, https://www.tandfonline.com/doi/abs/10.1080/07420528.2016.1236807?journalCode=icbi20.
7. Ryan Buxton, "What Seventh-Day Adventists Get Right That Lengthens Their Life Expectancy," HuffPost, July 31, 2014, https://www.huffpost.com/entry/seventh-day-adventists-life-expectancy_n_5638098.
8. Jesse Motiff, "My Love Affair with the Green Bay Packers,"

Bleacher Report, May 19, 2009, https://bleacherreport.com /articles/178741-my-love-affair-with-the-green-bay-packers.

9. Motiff, "My Love Affair."

10. Thomas Cahill, *The Gift of the Jews* (New York: Anchor Books, 1998).

CHAPTER 11: COMMUNITY IMPACT

1. Joshua Becker, "21 Surprising Statistics That Reveal How Much Stuff We Actually Own," https://becomingminimalist .com, www.becomingminimalist.com/clutter-stats/.

2. Kim John and Lisa M. Ross, *Simplicity Parenting* (New York: Ballantine, 2009), 57.

3. Acts 20:35.

4. Christopher Vecsey and Robert W. Venables, eds., "An Iroquois Perspective" in *American Indian Environments: Ecological Issues in Native American History* (New York: Syracuse University Press, 1980), 173–74.

About the Author

Jefferson Bethke is the *New York Times* bestselling author of *Jesus > Religion* and *It's Not What You Think*. He and his wife, Alyssa, host *The Real Life Podcast* and run FamilyTeams.com, an online initiative equipping families to live as a multigenerational team on mission. They live in Maui with their daughters, Kinsley and Lucy, and son, Kannon. To say hi or to learn more, go to http://jeffandalyssa.com.